The Delacorte Review

Issue 7

COLUMBIA UNIVERSITY
GRADUATE SCHOOL OF JOURNALISM

The Delacorte Review
Columbia University
Graduate School of Journalism

www.delacortereview.org

ISBN 979-8-76-803352-1

Independently published.

UNTO THE CHILDREN

CONTENTS

INTRODUCTION

You were not supposed to be reading this in print because by now print should have been dead.

That is what people wise in their own estimation said ten years ago and again five years ago. Print was over. The world was moving inexorably online and as it did, the tradition going back thousands of years of words and images on paper would vanish.

Except you are reading this on paper. Chances are you read a lot of words on paper. Many people do. In the first three months of this year, some 200 million print books were sold in the United States, an increase of about 47 million books over the same period in 2020. People bought all sorts of books, and high on the list, we were thrilled to see—given what we publish—was adult nonfiction, which accounted for 82 million books sold.

In fairness to the seers, it was reasonable to believe, though not necessarily to conclude, that as recently as 2012 print was in deep trouble. That year saw 591 million print books sold, a precipitous drop from a high of

778 million in 2007. But then print sales began to climb again and by 2020 some 750 million books were sold.

So what happened? Why is print not just alive but kicking?

Theories abound: the ebook market, robust though it may be, had peaked; it is much easier and less expensive to give a print book as a gift than a Kindle, to say nothing of adding a new volume to the bookshelf; and it is now understood that while new technology can overwhelm the old, the old never quite disappears.

But perhaps there is something simpler at play: the experience of print itself. Or rather, the miracle of it. Print comes without distraction. It reflects a choice: out of all my options I picked this book, this story. That means a commitment. And even if that book or story does not always live up to expectations, the time spent reading was done without interference. No swiping. No alerts. No Tweets. Often just the words on the page which, yes, miraculously have the power to transport you to someplace you've never been, where you meet people—real or imagined—who seemingly out of nowhere come to matter.

Even as the digital world offers all sorts of new ways for telling stories, so too is print proving itself to be alive with risk and possibilities. Words still matter. But so too do images, and words and images working together. Print offers an experience, one very different from those offered online.

For years we published only online. The decision was an economic one; print was just too expensive. But, ironically it is new technology that has made print affordable. We are not abandoning our online presence even as we embrace print, in all its new and exciting forms.

This means that no two print issues of The Review will necessarily be the same. Our first stab at print last spring replicated what we'd been doing online: five ambitious works of narrative nonfiction built around a theme, in that instance Loss and Hope.

This time, however, we wanted to try something new: three new original stories about parents and children, each very different. In her memoir, When Momma's Prayers Weren't Enough, Zenique Gardner Perry tells the story of returning home to be with her mother after her nephew's arrest for murder. Lawrence Tabak's A Headstone for Zach, is the tale of a journey he makes to the graveyard of East European Jewry as he mourns the death of his son. In their oral history, Forgiveness, Somayeh Malekian and Mahsa Afarideh recount their own stories, as well as those they've been told, about the endlessly complex relationships between Iranian mothers and their daughters. Their story is accompanied by an interview with the authors about what they discovered when they asked these women about one another.

We've also gone into our archives, to find sections of past stories that speak to the maddening, illuminating, moving, vexing, embracing, and eternally fascinating relationship between parents and children.

We hope you enjoy the experience. We'll be back in the winter with something new. What it will be, we do not yet know. Which is part of the fun.

Michael Shapiro, Founder and Publisher
The Delacorte Review

A HEADSTONE FOR ZACH

People told us that it would get better, the grief. But how was this different from forgetting?

By Lawrence Tabak

Three months after my pilgrimage to Poland in June of 2018, I received an unexpected call from a sales representative at Sunset Memorial Gardens in Madison, Wisconsin. He explained it was time to order a headstone for my son's grave. While we had a perfectly professional conversation on the phone, I broke down upon hanging up. It wasn't as if the call had been a shocking trigger. In that first year of loss I found myself facing crippling waves of grief daily, set off by any of hundreds of ordinary activities. This was just one more.

I sat at my desk and looked out at the beautiful fall Friday. On a day like this, in any of the past twenty years, Zach and I would have been taking advantage of the newly resurfaced public tennis courts around the corner in our neighborhood park. We would have been gearing up to watch our hometown Wisconsin Badgers play football. He'd have been up late working on his DraftKings picks for Sunday. All of that came to an end on Saturday night, April 21, 2018, when Zach, having finished a poker tournament, was struck by a car in the parking lot of a local bowling alley. He was twenty-six.

My wife Diane and I had planned on joining my brother Bob and his wife for the Poland trip months before we lost our beloved son, the younger of our two boys. Over the weeks following the accident, we'd asked friends and counselors if we should still go. None of them said no. So with heavy hearts, in mid-June we flew from Chicago to Toronto to Warsaw. Once there, cemeteries turned out to be key destinations. If you are Jewish and returning to search for your Polish roots, the two most likely destinations are death camps and cemeteries.

We noticed a theme among the graves: Some of the surviving memorial stones, most from the 18th and 19th centuries or the first forty or so years of the 20th, were in the shape of tree stumps; others had a stylized, broken tree as decoration. Our guide, Tomasz Wisniewski, the author of *The Lost World of Small-Town Jewish Cemeteries* and *Jewish Bialystok*, among others, explained that these were symbols of lives cut short. Although we hadn't discussed it in Poland, Diane and I both had been impressed with the artistry and poignancy of these traditional designs. When we discussed the call from Sunset Gardens, we decided we'd try to follow this tradition with our son. I sent the salesman a few of the pictures we'd taken in Poland.

The frequency of these broken tree motifs was a stark reminder of the harsh life of those times—and not just for Jews—before vaccines and antibiotics, in a country with rampant poverty. But in Poland, in the years before and after my grandfather and grandmother fled to America in 1921, life was particularly and calculatingly cruel for the Jews. In addition to natural deaths, many Jews, then ten percent of the region's population, had been killed in violent pogroms, attacks sparked by a dangerous stew of motivations. The foundation was deep-seated anti-Semitism based on religious animosity and otherness. Another factor was long-term covetous machinations calculated to diminish the Jewish population economically, while producing the opportunity for immediate rewards via pillaging. The end game: to demoralize the Jews into emigration and in doing so to root out what was considered revolutionary thinking, and ultimately "return Poland to the Poles." This thread of nativism continues, and in its modern incarnation has made Poland one of the least hospitable European destinations for modern immigration. The general attitude was expressed neatly by the pick-up college-age guide who helped us tour old Warsaw. "At last," he gushed, "Poland has become a country where we all speak the same language, all look the same."

Many of the worst of these attacks came in the late 19th and early 20th century, when Poland was part of czarist Russia. Despite optimism that Polish autonomy might make anti-Semitism a thing of the past, animosity towards the Jewish population only paused after WWI when Poland regained its independence.

Through the 1920s and 1930s, a steady increase in institutionalized anti-Semitism was demonstrated in stricter Jewish quotas at universities and such ignominies as "ghetto seating" for those who did get in (specified benches for any Jews at a lecture). Over these years a series of escalating harsh impositions on Jewish businesses were enacted into law, including state-sponsored and supported competition and the requirement to banner the business owner's name, facilitating the regular waves of boycotts of Jewish stores. Even more telling was purely vindictive legislation, such as a ban on kosher butchering, or measures that effectively eliminated the Jewish population from welfare benefits. It's no wonder that large number of Jews fled Poland. Many resettled in other parts of Europe; some went to Palestine and other destinations; but the largest number, like my grandmother Rachel and grandfather Gdalia, came to the United States. Some two million Eastern European Jews emigrated to the U.S. between 1880 and 1921, at which time new quotas began to stifle the flow.

Our Polish trip had been long in coming. My older brother and I had been talking casually about visiting the birthplaces of our paternal grandfather and grandmother for years. We knew that none of their descendents had ventured back. It was my brother, now a retired rabbi, who finally took the initiative, booking our guide Wisniewski and hotels, and later asking if we'd like to join his itinerary. My wife and I readily agreed. Now, as I packed, feeling increasingly emptied as the suitcase filled, I found myself apologizing out loud to my Zachary for leaving just two months after the last time we'd heard his voice.

The missing stones

If you are a Jewish tourist in Poland, chances are you will not see the actual gravestones of your ancestors—most of these are long gone. The Germans took them to pave roads, sidewalks, and to lay building foundations. Local farmers have been found using them as grinding stones. Depending on location, you may find an explanatory plaque, a few headstones left behind, even some that have been returned by the minority of locals with an interest in commemorating their former neighbors. Sometimes you just stare at an empty, walled field, knowing that the bones lie below.

It's no wonder that I wept there. On June 18, 2018, I was crying in a sprawling graveyard in Bialystok. My grandmother's hometown, Bialystok had been a bustling industrial town since the mid-19th century, a textile center where most of the major factories and virtually all of the merchant shops had been owned by Jews. It's the largest city in northeast Poland, with a modern population of nearly 300,000, just thirty miles from the Russian frontier. In 1939, on the eve of WWII, about 60,000 Jews lived there, constituting close to two-thirds of the population. Samuel Pisar, a Holocaust survivor, internationally acclaimed lawyer, and advisor to U.S. presidents, writes about his childhood in Bialystok in his 1979 memoir, *Blood and Hope*. He describes it from his family's position of affluence (his father owned one of the first automobiles in Bialystok)—"a bustling commercial crossroad" full of "political movements associated with reform socialism, Zionism, and revolutionary labor" which "mingled with the teaching of the Torah."

But in her introduction to the memoir of Puah Rakovsky of Bialystok, *My Life as a Radical Jewish Woman*, the Yale historian Paula Hyman notes that most of the Jews of Bialystok were impoverished by today's standards. As was typical across the region, this did not diminish the Jewish obsession with books and education, which for centuries had given the Jewish population the distinction of virtually universal literacy.

Children began long days of study at age four to six in *kheyders*, and moved on to Jewish or secular secondary schools. The region was spotted with prestigious yeshivas for Talmudic training of teenage boys. During my grandmother's childhood and adolescence and up until WWI, Poland was under the control of czarist Russia, and the secular schools, including the Bialystok high school, were taught in Russian. Jewish youth, as a result, were much more likely to speak Russian, in addition to their native Yiddish, than Polish. Jewish boys also were also instructed in Hebrew (the script used for written Yiddish); girls much less commonly. One telling anecdote: When Jewish children in nearby Ciechanowiec were first exposed to radio in the mid-1920s they were described as fascinated, even though they couldn't understand a word of the Polish-language broadcast.

By the turn of the 20th century, Jewish bookishness went far beyond the centuries-old focus on holy texts, via the sweeping influence of the *Haskalah*, the Jewish Enlightenment. The Jewish population of virtually every city and town in the Pale of Settlement, the broad region that is now western Russia, Poland, Ukraine, and Lithuania—the region where Jews were required to reside—took pride in their lending libraries, which offered Yiddish translations of the great works of literature from Shakespeare to Dostoevsky plus less elevated popular works such as Zane Grey's westerns.

The thirty two-acre Bagnowka Jewish cemetery we visited in Bialystok was ancient looking, uneven, shaded by mature trees. Of the original 43,000 gravestones, some 7,000 are left. Tomacz Wisniewski estimates that in 1939 there were up to 270,000 Jewish grave markers in Bialystok's numerous Jewish cemeteries, with just 14,000 surviving the war.

As I looked over the fields of gravestones and memorials, many of them half-buried or broken, I kept picturing Zach's plain, currently unmarked gravesite in the new Jewish cemetery back home, a flat grass field with a few recently planted saplings, just a few blocks from the only home he could remember. I closed my eyes and confabulated his presence, his physicality so familiar that I could pull this trick at will. I could feel him standing next to me, his voice still clear in my ears.

What I heard him say was, "Why are you so far away?" and then, "Have you forgotten me?" The pain of his words, his presence in the face of the reality of his absence, was crippling, compounded by my fear that he was fading by the day, that soon I would no longer be able to pull off this conjuring. People told us that it would get better, the grief. But how was this different from forgetting? Throughout Poland we'd crossed paths with Israeli bus tours. School trips to Poland are as routine for them as our tradition of touring Washington DC. The last Holocaust survivors are dying and the leaders of Israel, my age peers, also fear the forgetting.

❁

A few months after we returned from Poland, I took on the unwelcome task of completing Zach's last tax return. He'd recently started working full time at a local insurance company while studying for his third, challenging actuary test, reading up on topics such as "Put-Call Parity," "The Binomial Model of Replicating Portfolios," and "Modeling Stock Prices with the Lognormal Distribution." He'd always liked math and carried a school district ID he'd received to authorize his volunteer tutoring at the local high school. Our accountant was surprised to find a 1099 from DraftKings among his income statements. He said it was the first one he'd ever seen.

Zach took his gaming pretty seriously. Although his self-criticism when playing tennis or computer games was creative, loud, and often profane, he never had an unkind word for anyone else. At the extremes, he would recognize the absurd humor in these self-deprecations. In one high school tennis match he so thoroughly debased himself after a long rally his opponent felt the need to call out, "You do realize you won that point?" Upon which both players along with audience broke into laughter. He didn't hold grudges either, despite the shining examples his father set before him.

As we were straightening up the basement around that time, my wife pointed me to the dusty Nintendo Game Cube sitting in the corner with its maze of cords. "Should we see if one his friends wants it?" she asked. I choked up and could only shake my head. I was thinking of the day it had appeared. Zach had been around fourteen, his older brother just off to college. Ever since I spied my first Nintendo game console, I had been leery of what I assessed was addictive allure. We had forbidden the purchase of any of the subsequent game systems, imagining naively that our boys would instead spend the time exploring the outdoor world or reading. Zach had saved up his birthday gifts and spare change and walked a couple miles to the game store in the mall and bought the used Game Cube.

"You're going to make me take it back, aren't you?" he asked, when

I first noticed it. I told him no, that it obviously meant a lot for him to arrange the purchase and he was old enough to make the decision on his own. He soon began to improve his already considerable gaming skills, focusing on Mario Kart, in which Mario raced through various dream-like courses on a little go-cart. For practicing these races Nintendo had created a clever system in which a soft image of the gamer's previous best cart ride could be seen and chased. Gamers called these "ghosts."

In the summer of 2017, Zach announced he wanted to drive the 325 miles to Grand Rapids, Michigan to compete in a one-day Mario Kart tournament. "I think I can win," he said. "Unless a ringer shows up. Winner gets $1,200." Mario Karters like to post their best times on a website and Zach's times were clearly better than the past participants. His plan was to leave at four in the morning, drive up for the tournament and then drive back late that same night. By the time we'd worked out the details, he was taking my car instead of grandma's inherited 1997 beater and staying overnight at a hotel. He won the tournament handily, but only brought back a partial purse. Zach told us that the guy who runs the tournament—and who had, it turns out, won the previous events—didn't have the cash, "But he'd send me money monthly."

I warned him that he might never see that money, but the checks steadily arrived. So did Vincent, the tournament director, on the day of Zach's funeral. He was standing in front of the synagogue when my extended family arrived. My wife noticed him immediately as "someone who looked like a friend" and went over to introduce herself. He had driven the five hours—"because I had to," he said. Even though he'd only known Zach for a day. The summer after the funeral he held the tournament again, and renamed it "The Zach Tabak Memorial Mario Kart Tournament."

All of which flashed before me when Diane suggested we give away the Game Cube. I didn't know how to explain in that instant this whole story and how inside the Cube, on the hard drive, along with each of the Mario Kart courses, Zach's ghost was standing by, ready to race.

The Jews of Bialystok

There are no modern graves in the Jewish section of that Bialystok graveyard. For one thing there is scarcely a resident Jew left within a hundred miles. We were told that out of 300,000 people there were five known Jews. A 2018 survey by University of Warsaw sociologists revealed that 85% of contemporary Poles have never met a Jew in person. The few loose rocks perched on top of gravestones as tributes had been left by people like us: American tourists, Israelis, descendents of immigrants who had gotten away in time. As I wandered deeper into the cemetery, Wisniewski pointed out a ten-foot black marble tower, a memorial to the victims of the 1906 pogrom, an orchestrated multi-day attack on Jewish businesses and persons. The murdered were buried in this cemetery in a mass grave. Along with a Hebrew poem titled "Pillar of Sorrow," the monument lists the names of the official count of eighty-eight victims, although some accounts put the toll at closer to two hundred. Regular troops of the czarist army took part, with undisciplined Cossacks leading the way, backed by imported thugs, with the local police either passive or joining in. Many of the victims were shot, but much of the damage was done in more primitive fashion: Homes were invaded and looted, the inhabitants, including small children, beaten with clubs and tire irons or attacked with sabers. While repressed in contemporaneous accounts, rape was rampant.

This 1906 attack was hardly a singular event for the region's Jews. Even for Bialystok: Twenty-five Jews were killed in a military-led pogrom in July, 1905, and twenty-two were killed by military fire in October, 1905. It is hard, in modern America, to come to any terms with this kind of institutional violence from a standing army directed at a pacific and industrious minority. Perhaps the closest parallel is our country's awful legacy of brutality against Native Americans. And like Native Americans, Jews were regularly expelled from their homes and forced to settle in proscribed areas. And not just in Poland and Russia (Jews were expelled from Moscow in 1891): Over the centuries every European country had, at one time or another, expelled its Jews. And while the Holocaust overshadows all the atrocities preceding it, some 100,000 Jews were killed or wounded during the Russian Civil War pogroms of 1919-1920. In addition to sparking migration, the pogroms formed the backdrop for "the politicization of the Jewish masses together with the rise of the Zionist movement," as put by Jonanthan Dekel-Chen in his 2011 book, *Anti-Jewish Violence, Rethinking the Pogroms in East European History*. My grandmother, Rachel, was born in Bialystok in 1887 and would have been nineteen at the time of the 1906 pogrom. No family diaries, memoirs, or oral traditions exist to tell us what horrors she witnessed or personally experienced during those days; whether she successfully hid from the marauding, raping troops, or whether she was one of the surviving victims.

Rachel died at age fifty ("heart," said the cursory coroner's conclusion) in 1937, sixteen years after arriving in America, when my father was just fourteen. This eyewitness account of the pogrom by David Sohn provides a sense of what she might have suffered. It's excerpted from the Bialystok Yizkor book (one of hundreds of memorial books published by Jewish survivors and former residents of cities and towns across eastern Europe in the years after WWII):

> *Hundreds of hooligans armed with crowbars, knives and axes escorted by police and soldiers, fanned out into the centre of the city smashing doors and windows of houses and stores, looting and pillaging everything in sight. The unarmed Jewish population, terrified by these murderous acts, ran for cover in airless cellars and attics, where they hid for the entire three days, hungry and prostrate, anticipating death at any moment. The sound of gunfire echoed throughout the city. Armed soldiers and police went shooting in the streets and houses while bandits broke into and robbed the stores. On Thursday and Friday nights, the shooting increased...Either they shot people on the spot or forced a whole group out into the street and killed them there. Worst of all was when these vicious criminals gouged people's eyes out with their nails or stuffed their cut-open abdomens with feathers. Some of the victims included small children whose heads and other organs were removed. A particularly grim scene unfolded at the Bialystok railroad station where hooligans helped by the railroad personnel killed many Jewish passengers arriving on the train. The stationmaster laughed at this tragic scene.*

Two months later, this stationmaster was assassinated, part of a calibrated retribution by Jewish activists. And while there was little hope for Jews caught in the open by mobs or unlucky enough to step off the wrong train, it was not true that the Jewish citizens of Bialystok and other cities were passive. It was a common practice, when pogroms threatened, for Jewish leaders to attempt to intercede, often via bribes to city officials, including the police, and they tried to do so in Bialystok in 1906. Unfortunately, the local officials at the time were either not accommodating or powerless against the arrayed forces. Post-Soviet scholarship has uncovered definitive evidence that this pogrom and others were orchestrated by Czarist generals, no doubt convinced that Jewish intellectualism and Bolshevism were interchangeable. Jewish defense leagues had been organized in many towns, typically by the labor unions, and were capable of standing off the ordinary mob of ruffians and peasants behind a typical pogrom. But to deflect the full power of the well armed and organized czarist army was too much to ask of any rough militia, although the Bialystok neighborhoods with the strongest defenses (limited as they were to pistols and homemade bombs) were, with a fight, able to deter the troops and mobs, saving many from destruction. Perhaps my grandmother had been lucky enough to be a resident of such a neighborhood.

Later, from home, I read through the names inscribed on the Pillar of Sorrow. Among the victims were Israel Kustin, Moses Liberman, and Josef Burl, all aged three, and Jonah Kon and Avron Grynhojz, aged twenty-six. As I read this long list, I once again cried, thinking of them and their surviving families. Of my grandmother and her family under siege. Of my people. Of senseless loss.

April 21 had been a busy and happy day for Zach. I'd been at my desk around noon when he bounded past in the hall on his way to the bathroom, having completed one of his favorite activities: sleeping in on Saturday morning. I later found out he was racing to make the entry to one of the larger stakes poker tournaments of the year at the local bowling alley—$60 buy-in. It was the last time I'd see him alive.

After bombing out of the tournament, he'd switched activities by driving over to another nearby bowling alley to compete in their monthly pinball tournament. One of the pinball club members took a group shot that night, the last photo we have of him. He's wearing one of the "Poker Room" sweatshirts he'd won when the local Native American casino still ran games. We have a dresser drawer stuffed with them. Afterwards, Zach headed back to the first alley to put in some cash game action and was outside, getting directions to an after-hours game at a private home when he was struck. The paramedics arrived within minutes but never got a pulse.

From the main synagogue at the center of Bialystok to the cemetery would have been a long four-mile funeral procession in horse-drawn carts. That trip is no longer possible. For one, there are no synagogues left in Bialystok, even with its population of 300,000. The Jewish cemetery has been closed to any new prospects, should there have been any, since soon after the Nazis came to town in 1941, within days of their surprise invasion of their short-term ally, Stalinist Russia.

We made the ride from downtown Bialystok in ten minutes, stuffed into Tomasz Wisniewksi's Korean mini-wagon. Wisniewski is a professional historian, author, and filmmaker who specializes in the Jewish history of Poland, particularly in his hometown Bialystok and the surrounding towns of eastern Poland. He doesn't do a lot of tours like this, but he took us on, perhaps because the request came from my brother the rabbi. Perhaps he was also intrigued by our specific interest in our grandfather's city of origin, Ciechanowiec, about fifty miles southwest of Bialystok and about sixty miles west of the current Russian border. Or perhaps he was taken that my grandmother once lived and walked along the Bialystok avenues he knows best, like Suraska Street, where the Great Synagogue of Bialystok stood until the Germans burned it down on June 27, 1941 after packing it as full of as many Jews as possible (estimated at two to three thousand).

The Bialystok that my grandmother, Rachel Pogorelski, would have remembered from her childhood in the late 19th century was a city in transition, yet one which would have looked more familiar to a time traveler from two hundred years prior than one from thirty years in her future. Horse-drawn carts plied the streets; the bustling women on the sidewalks wore long dresses and traditional headscarves, similar in modesty but distinct enough in style to distinguish Christian from Jew. The businessmen of both religions hurried along in dark suits and brimmed hats. The traditionalist black-hatted, black-coated Hasidic Jews, a distinct minority of the Jewish population, would fit seamlessly into today's Williamsburg section of Brooklyn.

The Jews not only had their own houses of worships and schools, but their own bakeries and butchers, their own civic organizations and charitable aid societies, their own elected council of governors, even a separate court system. While assimilation of minorities, including the Jews, was a notion at times championed by both the Polish and Russian governments and by a segment of the Jewish population, it was not a popular concept with the Polish Christian majority who felt a God-given superiority over the Jews. They'd been taught by the Catholic Church that Jews were apostates who were responsible for the death of Jesus. The church, well into the 20th century, was also the occasional source of charges of blood libel, the bizarre but incendiary accusation that Jews would routinely murder a Christian child in the production of their Passover matzo. Nor was the prospect of assimilation popular with mainstream Jewish leadership, particularly the rabbinate, which quite correctly recognized the danger to its influence and to the integrity of their community that would likely come with full integration into society, as we've witnessed in the United States.

The 1900 edition of *The Jewish Encyclopedia*, written when the city's oral history still existed, has it that the Jews came to Bialystok in 1749 by invitation from the local royal, Count Branicki, who built houses and stores for them as well as a wooden synagogue. Rachel would have been thirteen years old at the time of the encyclopedia's publication, perhaps a student at the city's large Jewish school, the Talmud Torah, which served some 500 children. Prior to WWI, her family was financially secure, as her father had a position of responsibility in the textile industry. In addition to merchants and artisans (the mainstay occupations of Jews in Poland), an emerging class of successful and increasingly wealthy Jews owned the large mills and breweries and controlled the regional tobacco trade. My grandfather's family, who lived in a smaller city in eastern Poland, were likely employed in the tobacco industry at some point, since "Tabak" or its variants is the word for tobacco in Yiddish, Russian, and other European tongues, and occupations were a main source of surnames when they became required in the 1800s.

On Monday, June 18, our overnight in Bialystok happened to coincide with the concluding concert of the Eleventh Annual Jewish Cultural Festival of Bialystok. The festival has been run since its inception by Lucy Lisowska, the most prominent member of Bialystok's tiny Jewish population. The performer was Gerard Edery, a Moroccan-born New Yorker who was living in Warsaw. He is a self-described master of classical guitar and a former operetta singer who specializes in over-the-top performances of Sephardic Jewish music. The standing-room-only crowd, some two hundred people gathered in the grand ballroom of the Branicki Palace, absolutely loved him. This fascination with, and romanticization of, lost Jewish culture, which has become a cottage industry in Krakow, struck me as uncomfortably ironic, considering the historic efforts of Polish institutions to thwart Jewish culture. What to make of the enthusiastic applause for sacred Hebrew chants, bereft of understanding or context?

While we have no written or oral history of my grandmother's childhood and early adulthood in Bialystok, there is, by a wonderful chance—considering the small population and the absolute rarity of *fin de siècle* memoirs by women—a contemporaneous autobiography. This is not to say that *My Life as a Radical Jewish Woman*, by Puah Rakovsky, represents a typical experience for a female Bialystoker at the turn of the

20th century. Rakovsky was born into a financially secure family with a long and proud lineage of rabbis ("thirty-six generations") and was from an early age a child prodigy, a talent that was sometimes reluctantly supported by her family in a time where many believed the Talmudic proclamation that educating a girl was tantamount to encouraging licentiousness.

All of which makes Rakovsky's account of her early life even more enlightening, because the account of her teenage and early twenties is much less focused on intellectual development than it is on the rough-shod parental machinations and subsequent enforcement of arranged marriages for her and her peers. Intra-family alliances were particularly popular, and, at age fifteen, Rakovsky was promised to an uncle who was just two years older. When this fell through she was matched with a more distant relative, a great-grandson of a prominent rabbi. Despite her ardent opposition, which descended into a kind of depressive inertia, Rakovsky was married at seventeen to the rabbi's descendent and before her teenage years were over had two children. In addition to a clear portrait of a lack of women's control over life choices, one element that her memoir illuminates is the stark bifurcation of Jewish and Christian life in Poland. Despite being a gregarious and prominent member of society, Rakovsky describes her first personal relationship with a non-Jew occurring at age fifty-eight, when she visited her younger brother in Soviet Moscow and met his Christian-born wife.

What might have been

On Tuesday morning we left early for my grandfather's hometown, Ciechanowiec. We have no record of the family politics that brought my grandmother Rachel in Bialystok into a union with my grandfather, whose family members were prominent small business owners in this village some fifty miles away. It's likely there was some commercial association. One of the family enterprises in Ciechanowiec is said to be button making, which is cited as one of the town's specialties.

Ciechanowiec was very much a typical *shtetl* (Yiddish for small town) where Jews had been at its commercial hub for centuries. Yet by the turn of the 20th century the Jewish merchant and artisan class were not leading lives of economic comfort. In her memoir, *Sentenced to Life, A Survivor's Memoir*, Cecilie Klein observed that in a shtetl, "poor meant eating meat once a week, middle class three times, and rich every day." Families were large, infant mortality was high, childbirth was dangerous. Typical Jewish homes were small and drafty, heated by a central wood-burning cast-iron stove, which also served for cooking. Floors were more often than not packed dirt. A census taken near the turn of the century put average occupancy at five per room.

In early 2016 I immersed myself for two months in the Price Library of Judaica at the University of Florida in Gainesville. I was doing background for a novel I wanted to set in pre-War Poland. Although the specific citation has escaped me, I was much taken by the story I read of an American social worker who visited relatives in Poland in the 1930s. Having worked among the poorest of Americans in Appalachia, she was shocked to find her family living in conditions that were equal or worse in terms of material comfort, yet not in terms of culture. She described the Appalachians as mired in ignorance and superstition but was actually intimidated by the level of discourse at her relatives' dinner table in Poland. Everyone read multiple newspapers and was current on world events, and not only had a deep understanding of the sacred texts, but a familiarity with modern literature as well.

Meanwhile, as modest an existence as these small-town Jews led, theirs was richer than the farming population which surrounded them. Polish peasants, who constituted 70% of the population of Poland through the 1920s, were either tenant farmers or owners of farms too small to produce much more than sustenance crops. Not only was poverty rampant, but the peasants did not have the benefit of the social institutions that Jews built wherever they lived. An elderly Polish woman in Marian Marzynksi's 1996 documentary *Shtetl* is interviewed in Bransk, the next village down the road from Ciechanowiec. She's asked what is different without the Jews. Her response is that the Jews were constantly raising money for the poor, whereas, "In our community, if someone is poor, he gets poorer and nobody will help him." Polish peasants often pulled their children out of schools, when schools were even available, as soon as they could work the fields. Official figures from 1921 put rural illiteracy at 40%.

In a privately published family memoir, a nephew of my grandfather's, David Tabak, gives us the only written record of my ancestors' life in Ciechanowiec. From this we know my great-grandfather, Shlomo Shimon Tabak, was something of a *macher* (a big shot) in town. He had ten children with his first wife, who died giving birth to the last at age twenty-nine. Shlomo Shimon remarried and had four children with a second wife. (It's unclear how many of these children survived infancy, but almost certainly not all, since the infant mortality rate—death before age one—in Eastern Europe at the time was somewhere in the 20-25% range.)

Ciechanowiec was virtually destroyed in WWI and many Jews had to flee to nearby towns. The once prosperous Shlomo Shimon Tabak died during the war, destitute. The period after WWI was in many ways as difficult as the war years. In the year following the war, only 15% of Poland's industrial workers were employed. The Polish-Russian war of 1919-20 produced more destruction and economic chaos, even though Poland surprised the world with its victory and established itself as an independent country for the first time in more than a hundred years. The Bolshevik army occupied Ciechanowiec for a short time in 1920. When Polish nationals retook the city, Jews were broadly accused of collaboration and a pogrom ensued, with Jewish shops pillaged along with the standard accompaniment of beatings and rapes.

As tough as the early decades of the 20th century were for Polish Jews, no one predicted that their world was soon to be violently annihilated. Among the Jewish martyrs of the Holocaust listed in the Memorial Book for Ciechanowiec, Poland are nine Tabaks. They would have likely died when the Ciechanowiec ghetto was liquidated on November 2, 1942 or soon thereafter in nearby Treblinka. When my brother and I and Diane and sister-in-law Ruth pulled into town on June 19th we were almost assuredly the first Tabaks to step foot there in seventy-six years, and certainly the only Jews in town.

As we parked near the center of the city it was hard for me to match the scene of sunny, tree-lined streets and modern cars with my mental image of Ciechanowiec. As we crossed the street to the city offices I tried to imagine my grandfather, half my age, in long pants and white shirt with a tailored sports coat (Jewish tailoring being a major occupation throughout Poland), hatless—a modern man, walking these sidewalks alongside black-coated white-bearded elders; Jewish women in shin-length skirts, wearing a mix of fancy hats and modest headscarves; girls in long dresses and boys sporting their short-brimmed hats. I'd prepared this image in my mind, but couldn't place it here.

We parked just a block away from the former market square, now only partially ringed by modern businesses. The former importance of these twice-weekly markets could be surmised by the expanse: At least two football fields could be laid inside its borders, now circled by paved roads, the center spliced into parking spaces and tree-lined islands. Prior to WWII, these markets would be packed twice a week, with hundreds of Jewish merchants working their storefronts and table displays and peasant carts full of farm produce, caged geese, and chickens. The cacophony of bargaining, honking geese, the smells of grilling sausages and fresh baked bread, and the drifting odors from the nearby acre of parked horses would have been overwhelming. It's hard to imagine while gazing across the broad and quiet square.

Thanks to our guide's preparatory work our first stop was the mayor's office in a modern building with a red-tiled roof: *Urzad Miejski*— City Hall. We were greeted in English by the mayor himself—Burmistrz Miroslaw Reczko, who had studied in the U.S. at the University of Detroit and was pursuing a PhD in history from the University of Bialystok. Mayor Reczko had prepared a spot for us around a table in his office, with a bowl of fresh, locally grown cherries as a centerpiece. He's a six-foot-tall, middle-aged man, with bushy brows and reading glasses perched on the end of his nose. He had a serious mien, which matches his original career path into the priesthood

Mayor Reczko had graciously taken the afternoon off to show us his town's Jewish history. It was great fortune and quite unusual in small-town Poland to find a mayor not only conversant in English, but a historian with a particular interest in the Jewish history of his town. Small town modern Poland has not proven to be entirely hospitable to such pursuits. In nearby Bransk a Catholic city official, Zbyszek Romaniuk, found his similar interest leading to accusations of his own ancestry and a series of threats, including a Star of David carved into his door.

Small town and rural Poland is where the right-wing and nativist Law and Justice Party—and its current Polish President, Andrzej Duda—has its deepest support, not unlike the urban/rural political divisions in the U.S. Also, much like the U.S., small town and rural Poland has seen much less of the economic boom of the past fifteen years that has centered in the big cities and rewarded the educated. The mayor told us that the official population of Ciechanowiec was just under 5,000, about half of what it was pre-WWII. It is likely that the respondents of similar cities make up much of the 25% of the today's Polish population that believes modern Jews should be held responsible for the death of Jesus, and the 53% who concur that Jews conspire to control the world's economy.

Neither was small-town Poland, where the majority of Jews in Poland once lived, a sanctuary for them during the Holocaust. In May 2018 the Jewish Telegraph Agency previewed a book by the historians Barbara Engelking (Polish Center for Holocaust Research) and Jan Grabowski (University of Ottawa), which details how dangerous small Polish towns ("death traps") were for Jews. Places where "everyone knows everyone" were nowhere to hide or attempt to get by on false papers. Ciechanowiec also holds the sad distinction of being one of the many locales in which a handful of Holocaust survivors returned to their hometowns only to be attacked and murdered by their former neighbors, most often in fear that they would reclaim their houses and businesses.

From City Hall we walked a short distance to Ciechanowiec's former synagogue. It's a tall two stories, the bottom half weathered red brick showing some remains of white plaster, its upper level bricks still mostly covered in plaster. Only its arched first and second floor windows, unmatched elsewhere in town other than the towering Catholic church, hint at its religious backdrop. I was moved as we circled the building, letting my hand graze the bricks, imagining the hundreds of times my grandfather and his family had walked with Sabbath-best-dressed throngs through the city on Friday nights to come to the packed services. The Mayor stopped and pointed at the bricks at the bottom of the foundation. "We believe these date back to the 1600s," he said.

Under the Mayor's leadership the synagogue has been refurbished, including the installation of a new red-tile roof, and repurposed as the city's art center. A plaque near the entrance doesn't speak to the building's religious origins, but instead summarizes in Polish and English the Jewish presence in town since the 16th century: "From the 18th C. until WWII they comprised a majority of the town's citizens." And in a carefully worded statement that hedges the post-war tendency of Poles to absolve themselves from all Holocaust responsibility, the plaque ends, "In memory of the Jewish citizens of this land killed in the Holocaust by those who served the German Nazism." I looked down at the worn steps leading into the building and found myself saddened but honored to be able to replicate those countless footsteps, taken over hundreds of years.

The main floor, where the sanctuary once stood, is an open meeting hall. Upstairs is a wood-floored dance studio and a music room, where old and dented brass instruments dating back to WWII and earlier are shelved and still played. A previous Jewish tourist, touched by the reconstruction, had sent the mayor a family heirloom, a young girl's Hebrew report card from a nearby Jewish school, along with her picture. It is framed and hangs in the hallway of the second floor.

❁

My wife has carefully preserved similar mementos of our sons in a series of large scrapbooks. These include snapshots of little ten-year old Zach with a tennis trophy next to other finalists, in the same age bracket but, as was almost always the case, a head taller. Programs from the all-city middle school band. Ticket stubs from the Itzhak Perlman and Bob Dylan concerts we attended when he was fourteen. Although, like legions of his fellow nerdy contemporaries, his social skills were nil, we assured ourselves there was time aplenty for that. We'd allowed ourselves to imagine the pleasure of a future girlfriend or wife—even children, thumbing through the scrapbooks over Zach's embarrassed protestations. Who will ever care now?

After piling into the city's van, the mayor drove us across town, pointing out the boundaries of the WWII ghetto, where some 4,000 Jews were confined. Then on to the site of the Jewish cemetery, on uneven, rolling terrain. It was for decades following WWII bare of headstones. But under the Mayor's leadership, *matzevas* (gravestones) removed by the Nazis and uncovered during construction and renovation work have been returned. We saw some seventy in various condition, many with legible Hebrew, Yiddish, and Polish inscriptions. I was deeply moved that this Christian man had taken such a lead even though the dredging up of Jewish memories might not be popular among many of his constituents. It was probably a factor in his losing bid for reelection a few months after our visit. I hope my thanks conveyed the depth of my gratitude. My great-grandfather, along with many other ancestors, had likely been buried here.

In the years after WWI, unable to effectively collect taxes even from those who had the resources to pay, the Polish government printed money, devaluating the currency and sparking hyperinflation. In 1919 there were one billion Polish marks in circulation, two years later there were 229 billion. By December 1923, 125 trillion marks were circulating. Charity from relatives and Jewish relief organizations in America became fundamental to the survival of millions of Polish Jews. A U.S. dollar bought twelve Polish marks in 1919; by September 1921 it took 6,500 marks to buy a dollar. This economic crisis, combined with anti-Jewish violence, pushed more Polish Jews to emigrate. My grandfather and grandmother left Bialystok and boarded the *S. S. Mongolia* in Antwerp in January 1921, and sailed to New York.

When my father retired in 1988 I badgered him to write down some of his reminiscences, and he finally started putting some memories on paper. The one that captured his youngest years began with his trip to boot camp after joining the army at age eighteen, in 1941. For him, his life began the day he left his Yiddish-speaking house and began living as a full-fledged American. My grandfather, who struggled to survive in America via odd jobs, emigrated for a better life, especially for his descendents. He would have been astounded at how fully his grandchildren had fulfilled these hopes. I'd like to think he'd have been equally proud that two of us felt the need to return to see where he and his forebears had lived in a complex, challenging, and now vanished Yiddish culture.

The past is always a world beyond our reach, but for Jews visiting Poland, it is more than visiting a lost world; it's an exercise of suffering in the presence of a past erased. Like the loss of a son, it also inevitably leads to contemplation of what might have been.

What would Poland have become with the "People of the Book" as the 20th century evolved into the age of the knowledge worker? Would Poland have become a center of technological innovation, the way Israel has? Or would Poland's Jews have remained repressed and taken the first chance to emigrate, à la Russia's Jews? (There are now more Russian Jews in Israel than in Russia.)

On a similar tangent, I contemplate what our lives would have been with my son present through my final years, instead of those years having the defining characteristic of the aching absence of his presence.

In June of 2019 our extended family unveiled Zach's gravestone, his *matzeva*. It has a brown and green stylized tree arching across the stone, broken where the trunk expands into branches. It's exactly what we envisioned, even as it's the last thing anyone with a child would care to see. As we walked the graveyards of our ancestors in Poland we didn't realize that here was something we could take back with us.

Still, I can't say my feelings about our trip that coalesced as we visited the shell of my grandfather's synagogue, the graveyards missing our family's names, were wrong. Our trip to Poland, it turned out, was much the same as our trip home: a return to an empty house full of reminders of bottomless loss. 🦋

WHEN MOMMA'S PRAYERS WEREN'T ENOUGH

A Killing. And a Summons Home

By Zenique Gardner Perry

I found Momma on her knees many times that first month I was back home. Her prayers were never quiet, each one ending in wails and foreign tongues. Sometimes she repeated the same words over and over, incantations of *mercy, mercy, mercy, mercy, mercy or watch over him Lord, watch over him Lord, watch over him Lord*, urgency in each refrain. Whenever she'd go silent, I would tiptoe to her room, hold the door steady as I opened it slowly, softening the creaks as it widened inch by inch. Her back faced me, knees bent on small pillows, a lace scarf covering her head and spilling onto her bedspread. Sometimes, when she was still rocking, sobbing and murmuring into the mattress, I'd walk my steps back and close the door behind me. But the other times, when the side of her face rested on her prayer veil, her body slumped into the bed frame, I'd walk over to her, place my hand between her shoulder blades and bend down towards her ear. "Momma," I'd say softly, "why don't you come on and go to bed." She would ease herself awake, uttering an excuse: just this one other thing she had to do. Rest wasn't a thing she often consented to.

I realized early on that, though I was the one who came home to be with her, I didn't know how to *be there for* Momma. She was getting used to being back in her home after spending months away from it. I was getting used to being back home after spending twelve years in Philly. Though she'd housed us all temporarily over the years, Momma spent long stretches alone in her two bedroom bungalow. Yet there was a piece of all five of us in each of its corners: Zeffy's clothes in bins stored in the basement, things he couldn't carry when figuring out if he'd move back to Philly or try something new in Denver; Tishbi's drum collection covered in African cloth scraps leftover from the fabric I'd brought with me from my semester in East Africa. Momma saved small pieces of each pattern after sewing dresses and skirts and little cute tops out of the colorful Ankara prints; Zack's coats and winter garments, a 45mm in its case, his fancy watches and other accessories his main girlfriend couldn't keep for the eight years he'd be confined in a prison eighty miles up the interstate.

The things I left, Momma wore. Our bodies were always close to the same size and she enjoyed adding a bit of my flair into her own wardrobe: a marled sweater here, a vintage leather jacket there, some booties I'd passed down because "that kind of heel" had gone out of style. Whenever I visited, I would leave something behind because she'd complimented it, tried it on, loved it in a way that I knew I didn't need it no more.

My sister Von, though, rarely left Momma with inanimate things, things like clothing that could be unpacked and borrowed or furniture that could be used until it was reclaimed. Von was responsible in that way. Whenever she made moves—across the city or country—she packed her own things, she gave her stuff away, she carried it with her. But Von was a tornado. And the only one of us with children. What she'd often left with Momma was the responsibility of raising one of them: TJ, Von's firstborn and Momma's eldest grandchild.

Of the two rooms in her house, Momma had made one of them his. It was mine now. When I arrived, it took us a few days to pack TJ's belongings in boxes that she wanted stored in the basement. Though we both considered alternatives to keeping them, we ultimately abandoned those options, just in case something changed. Maybe he'd be released sooner than later and would go looking for his favorite polo shirt or the pair of Converse he wore when skateboarding. Maybe he'd need a suit for his hearing, the judge, upon noticing his necktie, would say, "This must be some sorta mistake." Momma prayed for such miracles, kept jars of water with his and Zack's names written on paper labels taped to its glass, a ritual as old as our ancestors, returning when her hands and knees weren't enough.

Two weeks after I'd moved home, Momma took me to see TJ at the juvenile detention center. Once we'd gotten past the glaring security guards, the metal detector and the dimly lit corridor that opened into the cafeteria where the confined children awaited their visiting loved ones, TJ, at first calculating his steps under the watchful eye of the correctional officers, reached for Momma and then me, holding us each in a long, breathless embrace. I smiled wide and patted my cheeks dry as we let each other go and found our seats next to each other at a round table, scooting our chairs as close together as we could.

Shortly after our greetings, as Momma and TJ started integrating serious stuff about TJ's case into our conversation, I learned about the hearing that would determine if my nephew would be tried as an adult. The St. Louis mayor had publicly promised the people that the consequences would be harshly doled out, eager to make an example of TJ and his friends. The hearing was scheduled for Monday, September 28, 2015 and Momma was expected to testify about the events that occurred the night of the incident. I was aghast at the news, mostly at the thought of Momma taking the stand. There were too many stories of the way Black folks, especially Black women, were reduced to nothing when faced with the lines of questioning in a courtroom. And now, because of TJ, my mother would be doing just that in five months.

But I said nothing at that moment. Momma, in performance mode, navigated with grace the ebbs and flows of this hour we spent with each other. She gleefully gave her grandson her full attention as he sat arm's length between the both of us and talked incessantly about the detention center art classes, the cars he'd recently seen in some magazines and his post-prison plans of finishing high school and joining the military. Then there was me, sitting between them, straining to be as present as possible. It felt like it was only me, straining to listen, straining to smile, straining to hold the immense anguish and the impending angst I felt rising up within me, for my mom and for all of us who'd been, at once, catapulted into crisis.

It was five months earlier on a Sunday afternoon in November. I was still in bed. The midday sun, clear of clouds, came through the curtainless windows and made my room so warm that I didn't have to adjust the fireplace beside me, mounted on the wall. When Zeffy called, I was reading an interview from the October issue of The Sun Magazine: a Black woman pastor, a lesbian, leaning into the Gospels, talking about her advocacy for the poor, for communities on the margins, the interview aptly titled, "Dangerous Love." I answered the phone knowing my brother would want to catch up about how we celebrated our respective Thanksgivings in the days before—his first in Denver and my first alone in Philly. Maybe we'd do some reminiscing on the one we spent together with most of our family in Philly just two years earlier. Maybe we'd eventually get around to talking about how shitty it was that the St. Louis courts didn't convict Darren Wilson for the murder of Michael Brown just days ahead of the holiday. But when I picked up the phone and greeted him, my brother didn't meet my enthusiasm on the line.

"Nique, TJ got locked up."

"Wait…what?" The air thinned. "When?"

"Early this morning. Like the middle of the night," Zeffy took a beat. "Nique. They say he killed somebody."

"What, no. No, no, no. Zeffy. No."

"Momma called me this morning. She said he said he got into a fight with a Bosnian who called him and his friends niggers as they were crossing the street. The Bosnian dude got out and tried to fight all of them when one of them hit him with a hammer. He ended up dying at the hospital, man," he sighed by the end of his telling. I was sitting up in my bed now, crying, in disbelief, my stomach in knots. I thought I would vomit.

"It's all over the news, Nique. They been saying it's a hate crime in retaliation of the news about Darren Wilson. The Bosnians are protesting all over Bevo Mill right now."

"Damnit, TJ! What the fuck?!" So many emotions welled up at once and I immediately wondered about my mom. How confusing this must be for her. How unsafe she must feel in her home embedded within the Bosnian community. I wondered if she would be vilified and her house targeted by the protesters. I hoped that her neighbors would shield her from the harshness, even though one of hers had killed one of theirs.

I had just seen TJ the month before. I brought my dog, Jaxon, to St. Louis to be with him and Momma as I made my way to an organizing gig in Alabama. TJ had just returned from a botched visit with his mom out in Los Angeles. Von and her second husband were raising TJ's little sister and a new little brother in a house in South Central. My sister had been courting the city for a few years and finally cemented her stay when she fell in love with an undocumented immigrant with whom she'd move in, bestowing upon them the titles of husband and wife and, together, parent her children and have him father another. TJ, newly sixteen, threatened this utopia she built with this husband. TJ reminded her of a decade and a half of false starts, failed unions, homelessness, heartache, and all the scarcity in between. They fought so much during his last stint on the West Coast that Von threatened to have him committed to a psych ward if he didn't leave California.

When I saw TJ, he moved through elation about my visit and Jaxon's arrival to dejection about his mom's most recent rejection, his return to St. Louis and his struggle with getting back into school. It was then that I noticed he had started talking with a Spanish accent, similar to the way his new stepdad talked. My brother, who had seen TJ months before when he went out to California to see Von and our baby sister, Tishbi, had warned me of some of the vices TJ had turned to. Zeffy told me about the weed and the pills and the cigarettes he'd found TJ with. Said he talked to our nephew and encouraged him to go back to school and stop smoking what he called dope. But TJ didn't let on to any of those struggles when we were together. And I didn't ask. My visit was an entire day long and we spent all of those hours together. He'd let me hug his neck, even though he now towered over me. I'd cup his face in my hands, even as his stubble pricked my palm. I noticed he was growing into a man and I noticed the trouble behind his eyes, but I never wanted to bring it up because I enjoyed so much his return to boyhood when he was with me.

❧

Von and I were pregnant at the same time. She and I, a little more than a year apart in age, would have our children within four months of each other. But I was embarrassed for myself and my parents. Two of their unmarried daughters, obviously fornicating and getting knocked up. The Gardner's must be running a whore house! the church folk would say, See! pointing their fingers at our family and our fall from grace. I kept the baby news to myself. Me and its maker devised a plan and, just before the summer of my 19th birthday, I walked past picketers offering me other options and entered a building that I would not exit the same.

I went home after the procedure. Then we lived in a red brick two-story off Antique Row. It was the first house Momma rented after she and Daddy separated. Von and I shared the largest room upstairs. Though Von was rarely home, she was sitting on her bed when I arrived, listening to music with the door to our bedroom patio open, the early evening sunlight brightening up the dingy white walls, a breeze moving between them. Von seemed to be illuminated by the orange glow of the early evening sun, her belly forming some roundness on her petite frame. She was wearing a pair of denim shorts that was left unbuttoned and a crocheted crop top that accentuated her breasts and stopped right above the bulge forming below them. Her blossoming body annoyed me.

I stood in the doorway, watching her for a moment before I walked in and turned off the stereo. I closed the patio door and retreated to my bed, keeping my clothes on and climbing under the covers, bringing the blankets over my head. Von looked up and, while glaring at me with righteous indignation, ran her mouth until I became undone.

"Momma! Something wrong with Nique!"

I was crying uncontrollably when Momma walked in. She stood in front of me, patience and curiosity in her eyes, and asked me what was wrong. I told her everything as Von looked on, this new knowledge shoring up some superiority she would hold over me.

"Thassa sin. I would never kill my baby."

"Von, get out of here. Let me talk to Nique."

As Von left, I started sobbing in Momma's lap. Von was right: I had sinned. And the shame that drove me to do it now overwhelmed me.

Momma let my tears soak her skirt.

"Why did you do it, Nique? Why didn't you come talk to me, baby?"

"I was afraid, Momma. And what would the church think about both of us being pregnant at the same time?"

"I don't care about none of that. We would have loved both of those babies. You know I don't agree with no abortions, Nique. It's a sin. You can always bring a child into this world and we'll figure it out. We will always find a way to love on that baby."

TJ was born midsummer. He was brown and beautiful from the beginning, his skin new, wrinkly, soft to the touch, his lips a puckered circle between his plumping cheeks. However, his perfection didn't pause the tumult that had grown between Von and his father. Their years-long, volatile love affair had become gravely untenable and, soon after his birth, they quit on each other, the burden of caring for a baby left with my 17-year-old sister. Her resentment would wind itself into the upbringing of her first child, her anger towards the father turning towards him, her need to hustle hard, using her body as a commodity, hindered whatever affection a mother would inherently have for a baby brought forth from her body.

It was Von and TJ who would put my mother's proclamation to the test.

❖

I read the police report soon after I settled back into St. Louis. Momma had given it to Daddy to look over before, maybe even read some parts of it to Grandma, but she spent some time processing her thoughts with me as I sat in the living room with the documents spread across the coffee table.

"They say they think TJ is the one who used the hammer. All the boys are blaming it on him. I think he got confused when he was talking to the officer. I just…I just don't know…"

I wanted to read it without her inferences, but I knew she'd been holding so many of these details alone for so long. Though I had yet to see her cry, I knew it was her sadness or despair, maybe guilt, that weighed her down. Well into the darkness of most nights, if she wasn't praying, I would find her sitting in the dimness of the den, only the light from the naked bulb of a small lamp on the corner table poked through the room's opacity. I often wondered how many times Momma replayed the scene in her head: Jaxon alerting her first, frantically barking when the bright lights from the police cars were cast on the house just after midnight. The banging on the door and windows that startled her awake. The fear and dread and shock. Police officers, too many of them, in her living room, towering over her, surrounding her, bombarding her with questions. Her questions: *where's my grandson? Is he okay?* The quickening pulse. Her quickened pace. Her hastily getting dressed to be escorted to the station. Her questions: *where's my grandson? Is he okay?* Their questions. Her prayers, the ones uttered out loud and in her head, *Oh God, oh God, oh God.* The confusion of who she's talking to. Who to talk to? Lawyer? *We don't have a lawyer.* "One will be provided for you." The few moments that she shares a room with her grandson. Her questions: *What happened?* Him slipping away. Hours later, emerging from the station in new daylight. The fear and dread and shock.

For the thirteen-plus years Momma inhabited that block, Bosnians, who fled a collapsing Yugoslavia and ethnic cleansing in the mid-'90s, were the residents of the homes on either side of hers. Momma's neighbors were parents who had become grandmas and grandpas since the time their children learned science and social studies in the public school where Momma taught; her former students, running into her at the corner store and still calling her Ms. Logan, introduced her to the babies on their hips and the husbands by their sides. These were families who knocked on Momma's door and extended invitations for weddings and memorials, baby showers and birthday parties, sometimes Momma returning home from these events with a covered dish of dumplings and kebabs and, only occasionally, one or two pieces of homemade baklava, perfectly crisped and sticky to the touch.

It was 2001 when Momma first moved to the neighborhood. She was teaching as Tishbi matriculated into fifth grade, both of them at the middle school two blocks away from the new house. Me and her other four children had dispersed into our newly-adult lives: Zeffy, some months home after serving in the Army, was riding around the state of Illinois selling insurance policies to veterans, mostly in rural, white towns that most of us wouldn't drive through at night. He rented an apartment in a suburb near the areas he frequented. With his erratic work schedule and long traveling days, he rarely visited us in the neighboring state. Von was stripping in seedy nightclubs then, also in Illinois. It was in between pole dancing and parading around those clubs with her bare breasts and in jeweled panties and stilettos that she met a sugar daddy she called Ralph, an old and lonely white man who acquired for her a Volvo and furnished a two-bedroom apartment in South St. Louis. Here, TJ stumbled into crawling and wobbled into walking, weaned off his mother's breast and watched and experienced his mom at war with the world. Zack, though still a teen then, had also left home. An older woman had moved him in and was teaching him how to be a man in the streets. He was running drugs and guns and whatever else while playing daddy with her kids, even as he needed his own father figure. I learned years later, after Zack came home from an eight-year prison sentence, in the middle of a therapy session that I had set up for him and that he'd ask me to sit in on, that our daddy's departure is what devastated him most. That he needed him in those years before he aged out of boyhood. That he often felt lost in the moments between the sheets of an older woman and the streets of the unknown. I cried on the couch beside him that day.

I was still in St. Louis when Momma moved to Little Bosnia. In fact, I was just returning to St. Louis from spending three months in a shipyard somewhere along the swamps of Louisiana while awaiting the completion of a river-barge cruise line. I had been hired to be part of its inaugural journey. But its completion date kept changing and, with each passing day in the cheap motel where they boarded us, I missed home and the boyfriend I left behind. When I got back to St. Louis, I moved in with him, a man fourteen years older whose manipulative and jealous tendencies became most apparent as I prepared my exit for Philadelphia two years later.

It was in those days when I visited Momma and she shared the stories of war that her students often broke open with. The horrors they fled and held onto were handed to her in the haphazard way trauma spills out of children, their growing bodies expelling grief and loss and rage in the most unlikely ways and places. This vulnerability—Momma's ability to add onto her burdens, theirs—was the kind of intimacy she established early on among a group of people who, in their initial relocation into this new city, a city that would brand them "refugee," was more foreign than her own blackness in the still segregated St. Louis of the early 2000s. And this established closeness was the thing that brought her back home.

It was after the news broke: "Four Black Boys Involved in Hammer Killing of a Bosnian Immigrant in Bevo Mill;" it was after they released

the names of the boys and after the pictures of the-then adolescents surfaced in places online when they couldn't appear in the papers; it was
after the Bosnian residents formed a televised protest, Momma's house
in the background, aggrieved men and women with their signs telling St.
Louisans that their community was now targeted by the Blacks in the
aftermath of Mike Brown's murder and the acquittal of Darren Wilson; it
was after Momma peered at them between the fingers that parted the few
blinds of her living room window, now alone with TJ's belongings, afraid
for rejection and retaliation, sorrow for the likelihood that there would be
no return to normal. It was the many days, then weeks, after the incident
when she made a trip back to the block to check on the house and pack
some things she needed during her retreat to Grandma Mae's, that an
elder of the Bosnian community, Ma Hadiya, would slowly stagger over
to Momma's house and find Momma at the edge of her porch. Momma
tells me that Hadiya leaned into her cane as she took Momma's hand and
covered it in both of hers.

"Meddy," Momma would tell me, mimicking Hadiya's accent and the
way she'd switch the lone "r" in Momma's first name to d's, "Come home.
We love you. This your home."

Momma didn't immediately tell me how she responded to Hadiya's
plea, but she told the story carefully, as if pulling it from the deepest place.

"That meant so much to me, Nique. That they didn't hate me…that
they didn't hate TJ. That made me feel like I could come back to my
house."

Still, Momma decided to wait until someone else could inhabit the
space with her, acknowledging that living alone in the house again wasn't
something she was ready to do.

My siblings and I all agreed that it made the most sense for me to
come home. We considered our options with Zack in prison and Von's es-
trangement. Zeffy had just signed a new lease on a house with his room-
mates in Denver and Tishbi was reluctant to return to St. Louis as she
had just started pursuing music in LA. I had been contracted to do some
organizing work for the Affordable Care Act and the closing enrollment
date and the subsequent end of my assignment loomed. It became apparent that I was the most likely and willing to be home to acquire a job
and support Momma financially, if needed. But what else we all knew, an
unspoken truth, was that when it came to caring for Momma, I also had
the same loving hand that she often extended to us when we needed her.
I wouldn't rattle her with questions and demand for them answers. I was

slow to criticism and knew how to be quiet alongside her, allowing harmony to be the thing that prevailed, allowing her to immerse herself in prayer, even if she numbed herself to the parts that hurt most while doing so. I could be patient with whatever she needed and whatever she sought for her own healing, her own peace.

Daddy didn't let no grass grow under my feet before he wanted to see me when I first got back to St. Louis. Before me and his wife ended our decade-long quarrel and during long weekend or holiday visits from Philly, Daddy and I would meet at this quaint little diner that he loved near his house on the Illinois side of the Mississippi River. This was considered the neutral ground between his and Momma's house. I knew I could always get him alone in this diner, away from the affront of his wife's scowl and my scarce words, him and his defeat, worn as close as his clothing, sitting between us. The diner offered neutrality in this way as well, affording us freedom to be our jovial, excitable, reminiscent selves. Just a daughter and her daddy.

When he made these diner dates with me, he was always hopeful that I would be on time. I hoped he hadn't closely scheduled another appointment or, worse, met me for breakfast before he had to report to the transit center. In cases when it was the latter, when I would arrive late and find him seated in a familiar spot, in his uniform, despondent, he would chide me about my tardiness and say "'Cause you late don't mean I can stay here late now with you, Nique. Those busses can't drive themselves…not yet anyway!" His gloom would quickly dissipate and together we'd burst into laughter at the thought of automated city buses on the routes where he complained about "the broke niggas that wanted free rides" and "those poor white folks who wanna get on the bus still actin like they better than erbody else." Somewhere in there, I'd assure him I won't be mad when he has to pop up and leave me alone with my plate of pancakes and, after that, I'd make false promises that I wouldn't be late again.

This time it was morning and he had nothing scheduled. I'd been back home for less than a week and had been in constant communication with him since leaving Pennsylvania and driving myself to Missouri. When we talked over the phone, he inquired about Momma, asking how it's been, the both of us returning to her house, being in the company of the other. It was a passing pleasantry then. But now, together, just the two of us in person, after he hugged me and introduced me to the waitstaff, a couple of elder white women who knew his name but weren't nearly as friendly to him as Daddy was to them, he asked me in earnest, "How's your mom?" I wanted to tell him that I didn't know if she was sleeping or eating at regular intervals. That Momma prayed too much and cried too little. That her faith was all-consuming. That her hopes often over-shadowed the hard truth: their grandson, my nephew, wouldn't be home no time soon. Daddy was a realist so I knew that he'd nod in agreement, offer a platitude or two to ease my angst. I also feared that something said to soothe me would come at Momma's expense. That there would be inadvertent finger pointing, an allusion to the idea that TJ's ordeal could be somehow pinned upon Momma in the same way the demise of their marriage was, especially among folks on Daddy's side of the family, even as Daddy's infidelities were long known, though easily forgotten.

I gave him answers he could hold onto without needing more words. "It's been fine, Daddy. We've been good. Packed up some of TJ's clothes. Moved some things around. I'm making the second bedroom my own. Jaxon's feeling like it's a return home." At the mention of my dog's name, his attention shifted, an apology for forgetting him evident in his voice.

"Jaxon?! How's my big boy?" It was as if my large animal were another grandchild.

"Oh he's fine, Daddy. I think he misses TJ, too." We both nodded our heads at that, a beat surfaced between our words.

"Daddy, did you read the police report?"

"Yes I did," he said, quickly, confidently, and shifted himself in his seat.

"Did you?" He took a sip of coffee.

"I did."

"Mmm. What did you think?"

"I don't know what to think. It was a lot."

"Yeah it was." He eased back into his seat, his back aligning with the cushion of the chair. Then he rested his elbow on the table, leaning his body into it and facing me. "You know, Nique, there's a lotta things I don't understand. Like why was this boy even out at night like this? And what was he even doing with a hammer in the first place? I know he was with some other boys but, I know my grandson…"

Daddy went on and on for a while about TJ's recent erratic behavior and how uncontrollable he'd become, how turbulent he was, how bro-ken he must've been. He also talked about how hard it was to see his first grandson in the detention center. How demoralizing it was to pass through the security system, checking in his personal items and getting patted down by a metal detecting wand or someone's open and stiff hands.

"I know what you mean, Daddy. It's so much harder to see TJ where he is, even though we've been to prisons before, right? It's just so different."

"So different! I mean, I go see Zack all the time and it don't bother me nearly as much. We make that trip down 'nere, I take enough money to get change and buy all the snacks your brother wants and then we sit there and play chess or Scrabble and just talk the whole time. I mean, I've spent hours there with him. And we talk about TJ. I tell Zack all the stuff TJ be sayin about coming home, like he ain't did nothing, like this ain't something serious he done did."

I saw the emotion rising up in him, some sadness, some anger. He was as hurt as I was for this troubled child in our lives. But I also wanted to ask Daddy about his role in TJ's collapse. There had long been finger wagging and whispers about how he'd allowed his wife, L., to do the thing she always did: reject his kids for her own, denying us the space within their house that she allowed hers, regardless of their shortcomings. I wanted to believe that there were greater barriers that prevented Daddy from taking his first grandson into their home, especially when that was the thing that was expected of him after he'd gone to LA to extinguish the fires his daughter had started.

A year and a half earlier, Von found herself in LA with her husband, her children and our two siblings, Zeffy and Tishbi—all of them desperately trying to rein in the tumult of this growing and increasingly anxious teen that belonged to us all. TJ had filled out into a newer body of long legs, square shoulders, and a handsome face framed in a boxy jawline. It was early August and I was attending a writing residency in Lagos, Nigeria when I FaceTimed TJ on his birthday. He had turned fifteen-years-old and Tishbi and Zeffy had taken him from South Central LA to a hotel in Burbank for the weekend. The three of them crowded into the rectangular screen baring their teeth and singing songs. We laughed and marveled at the miracle of technology, its capability allowing us to be together on such special occasions, despite the miles between us. I took a screenshot to document the moment, posting it on Instagram to share with friends our love, our commitment to our first nephew, our presence in his life.

After spending three months in Africa, I returned to Philadelphia in mid-November. Zeffy, also returning to Philadelphia a few weeks after me, would be the one who'd tell me about the mayhem that unfolded mere days after our family FaceTime. On a winter night months after the ordeal, Zeffy sat across the dinner table at my house in West Philly and described in great detail the day a woman from California Child Protective Services showed up at Von's house demanding that TJ be surrendered to her. Zeffy, who had been living and working in South Philly at the time I left for Africa, had gone out to LA ahead of TJ's birthday because he had heard about TJ being hospitalized due to a failed suicide attempt, an event that no one bothered to disclose to me while I was traveling abroad. Apparently, after his suicide attempt and stint in the psychiatric ward, TJ had been mandated to attend therapy sessions, for which he hadn't been present for any sessions—or my sister had failed to get him to them. These absences prompted CCPS involvement.

TJ was removed and immediately placed in a foster home and a series of court hearings to regain custody of our teen was scheduled in succession. Zeffy called the court hearings a family affair: him and our brother-in-law, Von and their one-year-old son, and our baby sister, Tishbi—all of them, waking up early and piling into Von's husband's white pick-up truck to get to the city court building well before their case was called. Zeffy said that sometimes they would sit for more than an hour in the hallways, hordes of children amid the colorful toys and play pens, their families and caseworkers passing through, all of them awaiting a judge or jury to determine their fate.

It was at the second custody hearing that Von came up with the idea to tell Daddy to come and get his grandson. Von purchased a roundtrip ticket and, within days, Daddy flew out for his first-ever visit to the state of California under the pretext that he'd be the one saving TJ. Daddy spent one full day in court, making promises to the judge that TJ would be in his care and signing the paperwork to seal the deal. Daddy flew home the next morning and, a week later, the Tuesday after Labor Day, Zeffy said, is when the courts surrendered TJ to them. Von, eager to get her child out of California, subsequently arranged for Zeffy to take TJ to St. Louis where Daddy could fulfill the promises he'd made in court. And that's when the two of them, uncle and nephew, took a three-day train ride halfway across the country where, upon arrival, TJ would face rejection once more.

Zeffy said it was L. that barred TJ from coming to Daddy's house. And whenever Von or Tishbi talked about it, they spat it out of their mouths like bitter fruit.

"L. don't want nobody staying at they house but her kids. Set TJ right out and he'ain have no place to go BUT back to Momma's. Thass how he got in all this trouble he in."

"All this trouble" meant TJ's growing penchant for drugs, his disinterest in going to school and his longer, later nights spent in the street. He couldn't be restrained when he got back to St. Louis. And Momma stood in the way of any means of discipline for this grandson that she doted on and loved blindly.

"Momma wouldn't let me do nothin' with that boy, Nique. He was out of control." Zeffy, shaking his head and sucking his teeth while telling me this, admitted that this was the reason he returned to Philly after I got back from Uganda.

"He was gone, Nique. And there was nothing I could do. So I just came on back to Philly." Zeffy stared down into the table and silence swelled between us. I wondered more about what he'd seen and what I'd missed. I wondered if I should be thankful that I was absent during all the drama, because I never felt that kind of relief.

Almost two years later, while Daddy and I sat beside each other, a coffee cup in his hand and a full plate of breakfast in front of me on the table, getting cold, I wanted to ask him myself why he didn't keep his promise. Why he hadn't brought TJ to his home, enrolled him in school and became the guardian he was supposed to be when TJ returned to Missouri. I didn't ask Daddy that day, but I had an opportunity later to ask his wife, L. As is her nature, L. was short and to the point with her response.

"I couldn't deal with TJ. I just couldn't do it. I told Mary and I told yuh daddy: he'll tell the courts in California we'll take 'em, but when he get here, he can't stay at our house. Nooo, buddy. I couldn't do it, Nique. I couldn't handle him. He was too much...and I couldn't deal. And see what happened, don't you? Just like I thought. He was outta control."

And just like I'd thought, everybody had been right about L. Whether the decision she made to deny TJ had been imagined or heard as explicitly as I had, she was indeed the roadblock to TJ's refuge with my father. It brought me no solace to know undoubtedly that she refused our growing boy a safe place to stay, a father figure in his grandpa, and the boundaries of their strict Christian home, especially when I knew that she and my father had extended this kind of support to L.'s teen granddaughter, L.'s elder niece and, finally, L.'s niece's young son, regardless of the baggage they brought with them into their home. Daddy's children—us—and our children—TJ—weren't worthy of the space Daddy and L. made for hers.

But these aren't the places me and Daddy went when we met in the diner on that particular day. At that moment, with the unraveling of a family, the tearing of the seams, the burden of holding it all together being disproportionately distributed into the hands of Momma not yet made evident to me, I held for Daddy the same tender space I was holding for Momma and desiring for myself in this great big loss we were tethered to.

❁

At Momma's house, there was no room and no time to point fingers, to criticize, or to play "I woulda, coulda, shoulda." There was only planning and prayer. When I brought up in conversation what I knew folks were saying, what was happening in the news, or what family members weren't doing and needed to, she sat quietly. She didn't have it in her to argue about the aloofness of my siblings, the disinterest of TJ's mom, the hands-off approach of Daddy and anybody else who had nothing to offer but more helpings of blame and shame. What I eventually understood was that what she needed from me was to keep my badmouthing and brooding to myself. Momma was on a mission. And what I eventually understood was that what she needed *most* from me was to assume the position of her right-hand woman.

The first time Momma met Matt in person was during a visit to see TJ. Matt had been assigned to TJ's case promptly after the incident. By mid-December he had called Momma to introduce himself. By that time, though, she already knew quite a bit about him because she had quizzed the white woman who phoned her to tell her about the public defender for our family.

Who is this man? What are his qualifications? How long has he been practicing law?

Somewhere among these inquiries, the white woman on the line disclosed to Momma that the man was Jewish. Somehow, as maybe the white woman knew, this eased Momma's mind. It was the thing she hinged all of her hopes on when she talked about Matt's advocacy for TJ.

"Well, Nique, you know...he's Jewish, so I feel like he really has TJ's back. And he really seems to care about this case."

Then she'd lower her voice as if telling a secret meant to be kept just between us.

"He really feels like what TJ and the boys did was in self-defense."

I listened to her, offering head nods without saying nothing else. I didn't trust any of them, especially when I knew this was free work. Charity. Even if they did mean well, I was certain they were fighting for five or six or more Black boys just like TJ and feeling overwhelmed or exhausted or apathetic. I knew that it was tragic that we had no money for a defense lawyer, that our child was basically fatherless, basically motherless, living with his grandma in a house that was rented and not owned, with a car that was old and unpaid for. That we were Black. The latter our greatest burden, but in naming the other factors, makes that fact loom less large.

Matt told Momma she'd be a character witness for TJ when she took the stand.

Tell a story of the baby boy you love, the loss he's felt between his two parents, his searching, his great sadness. Tell them about the abuse and neglect, the fending for himself he often had to do. Tell them he sometimes wanted to disappear, sometimes dreamt of offing himself.

Don't tell them about him being kicked out of schools, about the underage drug and alcohol use, his easy access to these substances and the bad company he kept. Refrain from saying he regularly stayed away from home and there were nights you worried about where he was. Don't mention his erratic behavior and angry outbursts, the way you were sometimes afraid, for him and for yourself.

I imagine that this was how Matt coached Momma. And if that was what was asked of her when she was questioned in court, she would have aced it. Not because of Matt, but because of her own convictions, what she believed or what she remembered, the romanticization of the grandson she loved after he was taken away from her. The infantilization of a teen child when he is at his most vulnerable and in need of our hands and our help.

But, as it turned out, Momma didn't need none of what Matt asked of her. She'd later say, in his defense, that he told her to prepare herself in that way to present a kind of distraction, to give her something to focus on as she spent those months readying herself for the unknown. It was a benevolent read on what happened, a belief only Momma and her loyalty to a person in whom she put her trust could muster.

On the day of the hearing, I hardly slept. In my phone's archives is a 6:34am text to a friend that reads:

"The hearing for Travis is this morning. Please take a moment to pray for us today."

On the other side of my bedroom door, I heard Momma quietly moving around the house. She wasn't on the phone or in prayer or singing a spiritual or gospel tune to prepare her for the day ahead. While I'm sure she had prayer lines that extended beyond St. Louis, people of faith petitioning God from coast to coast, she became a solemn warrior that morning, preparing for a battle she knew was a losing one.

I remember working that morning, presenting a workshop at a school and rushing to the courthouse directly after. I remember my nerves the entire drive there, an anxiety rising up in me as I parked, as I passed through security, as I searched the hallways for the room, its old, ornate wooden doors, my mom and my nephew behind them. When I finally found the courtroom, the hearing had already started. I remember not being able to enter immediately—not because I wasn't allowed, but because my body was unwilling. I remember the way tension swelled in my belly, pushed into my muscles, made me feel as if vomit was its only relief. There was a bench in the middle of the lobby floor, directly in front of the doors to the courtroom where, initially, I sat, twitching and fidgeting, getting up every minute or two to peek inside the long, slim windows in the center of each of the double doors. The courtroom was packed. The victim's family, other Bosnians, friends and community members from Little Bosnia, a lot of them present and seated on one side of the courtroom. Daddy and L. were there, seated close to the front and on the side of the defense. I didn't see Momma or TJ in those moments, although I was certain they were both there.

I remember that on the times I looked in, there was a different person on the stand: a police officer; a young white woman, presumably the victim's girlfriend who was with the victim on the night of the incident; a correctional officer whom I noticed from the Juvenile Detention Center where TJ was being held. Finally, after a long time of pacing and waiting outside the courtroom walls, I peeked inside one of the long windows and saw Momma on the stand. I hurriedly and quietly opened the courtroom door and shuffled into an open space in a nearby bench on the defense's side. My body was riddled with a dull tremble.

I remember hearing and losing the questions as they were asked and only focusing on Momma's responses. Her voice, smaller than I had ever heard it, was also calm and measured. Her answers were solely about what happened that night. I remember her telling the court about how deeply she slept and that she didn't even know TJ had gone out. I remember her repeating that detail once or twice more. I remember her descending from the stand and taking a seat, perhaps where she was before. Though still unsettled, my body felt slightly better regulated.

I remember Matt talking next. It was my first time seeing him and he looked like a young, rookie lawyer, fresh out of law school and taking his social justice convictions to task on this case involving my nephew. He argued, as he'd promised Momma, that the boys were defending themselves against a grown man who was skilled in martial arts. Matt outlined for the judge and for everyone in the courtroom what details we already knew about the event: the victim allegedly yelled a racial epithet, the n-word, at the boys as they were crossing the street; somehow the victim stopped the car, exited the vehicle, and a fight ensued; during the fight, one of the boys brandished a hammer and hit the victim upside the head, fatally injuring him; the boys fled. Matt urged the judge to consider the ages of the boys, the rage that consumed them upon hearing the word, the plight of the city, the incident happening days after Darren Wilson's exoneration, and the victim's proficiency in martial arts.

The judge, Jimmie Edwards, a Black man and St. Louis native, could not be convinced. He gave a brief speech after Matt's, condemning him for bringing up the expletive, and chiding my nephew and his defense team for even considering it as a reasonable excuse for the loss of life. He talked as if the killing was deliberate and, shortly thereafter, before slamming his gavel down on the desk, made the determination that TJ should be tried as an adult. The hearing was over. TJ stood and it was the first time I saw his face that day, in plainclothes and with confusion casting a shadow over his face. He would shift from the Juvenile Detention Center to the adult jail downtown before evening. He had been seventeen years old for a month and a half.

Leaving the courtroom was uneventful. It was when I got in my car and drove across the Poplar Street Bridge and called my friend, when I heard her voice on my Bluetooth, reverberating throughout my car, that I started bawling. Sobbing in heaves. She told me to pull over and take some deep breaths. She told me she understood and to keep breathing. She stayed on the line and just let me cry. She knew it was the only place I could.

When I got home, Momma was there preparing some items for TJ, things she didn't know if he could even have at the adult jail or not. We didn't talk about anything that first night, even though we ate our meals together and sat in the living room together as we normally did.

For two days, she remained as quiet as she had on the morning of the hearing. I hadn't even heard her praying in her room or around the house as was her daily, several times a day, routine. Maybe she had finally grown angry at God. Perhaps she noticed this as her "Job" moment and resisted going to the Lord in prayer. I wanted so desperately to figure out her stoicism. How I'd cracked and she hadn't.

But it was in the quiet of that evening, those two days after the ordeal, as we sat in our respective places in the living room: her in the champagne-colored wingback chair and me, in the center of the white couch that was covered in plastic. This, too, had become a part of our daily routine: us two little ladies in a bungalow with our big dog resting comfortably on a piece of furniture nearby. Maybe I had asked her something. Maybe, in a moment of courage, I wanted her to process what she was feeling and I articulated exactly that. Or maybe we said nothing at all. And still, she noticed that what she held for months could not be held no more. She noticed that prayer could no longer be an anchor for this massive grief. She noticed, she noticed, she noticed. And she gave in.

Momma wept. 🕸

FORGIVENESS

Mothers and Daughters Search for Each Other in Iran

By Somayeh Malekian and Mahsa Afarideh*

There have been so many paragraphs, anecdotes, general news about the world, or other things that I thought of as the beginning to step into my side of the story here. But, as all adult life is about, making a decision and picking one out of the options is what defines who we are.

And it seems that with this beginning, I am seeking your understanding and eventually your forgiveness. Forgiveness of what, I do not know yet.

—SM

Maha, 43, Poet, Tehran

I'm dancing with my friends. I think it is my birthday party. Maybe it's just a gathering. I am drunk. I am absolutely happy. Suddenly the door opens and my mother in black veil enters the room and gives me a hard look. She definitely is going to kill me. I am not wearing a hijab. I am surrounded by boys. My heart starts pounding.

And I woke, shaking, sweating, breathless. Again, that hunting nightmare which probably won't leave me till I die.

I remember exactly the day it started. I was five years old. My cousins and I were playing some stupid game. They made me a bride, redded my lips with a colour pencil. One of the kids said let's go out. As soon as I stepped out, I saw my mother walking down the alley. She gave me the same stern look that still appears in my dreams. I ran back to the house.

I'm now 43 years old and afraid of posting a single picture of myself without a scarf on Instagram. So I wonder if I have religiophobia. I know how religious beliefs can harm children, especially girls, in a religious family.

It was during the Iran-Iraq war, which started with Iraq's invasion in 1980 and lasted for nearly eight years. Every Monday night we gathered in front of the TV and watched *Oshin*, a Japanese television drama about a miserable woman who suffered all the bad in the world. Sometimes during air raids we had power cuts and had to run to the basement. The first thing I did was get the radio so we could listen to the sound of our favourite serial being aired. When the characters didn't speak, it was nerve racking. We had to just imagine what was going on.

The cartoons we watched on TV during those years were not any better. I wonder if it was a kind of strategy, so we suffer less from our miseries knowing that there were more miserable people out there.

According to Islam, girls since nine have to follow the Islamic rules, boys since they are 15 years old.

So when I was nine, I had to fast during Ramadan. My father was fighting on the frontline. We had to go on with small sums of money. I was suffering from malnutrition. To make the matter worse, I desperately missed my dad.

There is a rule that says if fasting is harmful for your health, not only do you not have to do so, but to fast is a sin. My mother said it was my responsibility to decide whether I should fast or not, whether fasting would harm me or not. Because she didn't want to be responsible for putting me in Hell in the afterlife.

Back then, I didn't know what I should do. I fasted for the whole month, and at the end I got so sick, I was so weak that I barely could walk to school. For a while I would often faint. When my own daughter was a teenager and at some point she was in a religious mood, I forbade her to fast.

It has been more than a month that I haven't seen my child. Amid our marital problems, I applied for divorce, and he started to take our daughter to his brother's house every day when he went to work. Throughout the process, my husband took our child and wouldn't let me see her. During the years of our marriage he was not willing to look after her even for one hour. When I desperately needed to go to the dentist, for example, he would ask the neighbors to look after her. Now he was hiding her from me, as if I could kidnap my own child.

I remember crying to death at nights, holding her clothes tightly to my chest. It is how I missed her.

According to law, I am entitled to custody of her before the age of seven. She is four. When I went to family court seeking help they said it was absolutely my right to see my child, but they couldn't do anything about it. It was my own job to convince my ex husband. So one day I couldn't bear it anymore and I went to the door of my ex brother-in-law.

They didn't open the door. But I knew they were at home.

I went to a car repair shop nearby and bought some gasoline and a match box from a supermarket. I emptied the bottle all over my clothes and with the match in my hand I went back to their door, knowing they could hear me. I shouted, "I want to see my child. Either you let me in or I will burn myself alive right here in front of your building." When the neighbors started to gather around, my sister-in-law finally buzzed me in. My poor baby was playing alone in a room. I held her in my arms and as I headed to the door my sister-in-law locked us in. I went to a small balcony. Now I was literally kidnapping my child just because I missed her. I cried for help. I held my child from her armpits and gave her to some neighbors on the street. Then I climbed over the waist high bar and jumped down.

Since I had left my husband, I rented a small apartment. I thought that he didn't know where I was living. When we got home I changed my clothes and lay down in the bed with my child. Suddenly there was someone at the door, ringing the bell constantly. I looked through the peephole and my heart shuddered. It was him.

Later I found out that he had asked his brother to follow me from my work. Now he was banging vehemently on the door. I thought it would break into pieces. How had he entered the building? (Later my neighbors said they buzzed him in because he had claimed he was from the gas company.)

I called the police. When they arrived they took us to the police station.

There, officers said, "We don't want to interfere in your family issues."

They simply took the weeping child from me and gave her to her father.

As I walked home, it was getting dark. I crossed Azadi (Freedom) Street crying silently without paying any attention to speeding cars, thinking if only I was lucky enough to be run over by a car...

Somayeh Malekian, 39, Journalist, Tehran/London

It was my first session with that therapist, Ms. M. I was led to a small room with two chairs, a table, and a tissue box on it. There were no decorative objects in the whole room or on the walls except for a small frame hanging on the wall with a sentence I will never forget: "Understanding everyone is forgiving everyone."

I was born in a small room of an old house at the end of a long, dark dead-end alley which was not asphalted at the time and would become muddy all of the fall and winter. It was a big house with a huge yard in the middle and around six or seven rooms around it. There was a stable for the two cows of the extended family where some sheep and lots of hens were also kept. I remember two turkeys among the herd as well.

"Tell me if your mom now has a little niece or a little nephew," my dad asked his own little niece after I was born, just to know if his kid was a girl or a boy. As is tradition, he had not been allowed in the room where my mom was giving birth to me. And even after having two sons before me, my dad remained shy about asking my grandmother or the midwife the gender of his third baby. Anything with the slightest connotation of love-making is wrapped in shame, such that a father will not ask about his own newborn baby.

We are five. Though I make this tense mistake. We "were" five siblings before we lost our third brother in a terrible bus accident about eight years ago. Now we are four, me and my three brothers. Mehdi and Ali are older and Hossein is younger than I am.

Sona, 20, social work student in Europe
As told to Somayeh

I was born in 2001, a second child of a Turk family in Shiraz, a beautiful historical southern city in Iran. I can't remember much from the house where I was born. But I have heard it was a very tiny place filled with stuff our relatives had gifted to my very young parents so they could keep up with their tough financial situation. My uncle had brought a small electronic heater, the other one some blankets and dishes.

My mother was 18 when she got married to my 22 year old father. She had lost her own parents at a very young age. Her marriage had been a way to move from her father's house, where she took care of her younger siblings (since the death of her parents).

The last year of her high school, my mom sold sandwiches she had made at home to help my dad make ends meet. She got pregnant with my brother Soroush when she finished high school. She still tells the story of sitting at the nationwide university entrance exam when she was pregnant with my brother.

I was born four years after that, and it seems that their life started to boom since then. My father got a proper job in the oil industry in the south of the country and my mother started to spend more time with us.

I had a happy childhood filled with lots of memories of joyful ceremonies at school and spending time with friends. The oil company was famous for providing many facilities for the employees. Besides many often cheerful celebrations for any random reason at school—which is not that common in normal schools in Iran—we used to get so many presents at school from books to toys. I remember that my father would also get us many books. His favorite was one he had purchased on one of his trips to Malaysia. It was an English picture dictionary for children. So, at night, when he wanted to put me to bed, he would read me English sentences and translate them for me. I knew no English at the time. Now, in retrospect, the beauty of those nights is doubled when I remember that years later, it was me who would read English books to my father, helping him with translating the parts he did not know.

As close as I was to my father, I always struggled keeping my distance from my mother. I wanted to stay away from her, no matter how hard she would try to approach me on different occasions in my childhood, through my teenage years, and even now that I am 21.

I know that she herself went through a lot in her childhood after my grandmother's death. Maybe it is why she always wanted to be supportive to me. She wanted to be my patience stone. She wanted me to trust her enough to tell her about the first time I was dating someone in high school. But I always resisted. I could never trust her.

Unlike her family, who are all conservative and traditional in every regard, including anything related to women, my father's family are very open minded. It was a strange paradox.

By any means she tried to buy my trust, but I always and still resisted. I rarely hug my mother and only kiss her once in the New Year and once on our birthdays. That's it. This is the distance I defined.

It is strange enough as I was the closest person she had. I have always been the person who fully knew her and understood her, who could see the depth of her pains. All the pressure she would constantly endure from my father's family. Her determination and commitment to make sure everything is in good shape at home from preparing three fresh meals every single day to setting up the home and arranging all school-related things.

But with the palpable tension persisting in our house, her attempts were never enough to cut that distance short. Recently, I have started to get more distant even from my father.

There is something that I have started to deal with, it originates from a very young age. My parents were cheating on each other at the time and I knew that. It was so bad that I knew everything since I was around six, before going to school. My childhood and teenage years were living in the intervals of feeling anger and hatred towards my parents and enjoying my time filled with cheerful moments spent with my friends.

I still remember the day that I later realized was the moment my mother found out that my father was cheating on her. I was only four. It was full of shouting and breaking dishes and throwing phones and stuff at each other. I clearly remember the details as I was standing at a corner watching the scene in shock.

At the time we were living in Lamerd, a small town in the south of the country where my father got a job. There was a young woman, a second cousin of a relative or something, who was studying in Lamerd University and used to regularly come to our house as we were the only relatives she had in town. I liked her a lot. She was young and kind and would play with me anytime I asked her.

Until the night there was a big fight between my mother, father and this girl. I wasn't in an age to understand what was going on. But I got the deep hatred between my mother and her. My only question that night was why my mother was fighting her despite knowing how much I liked her and how kind she was with me.

Even if I would not miss any chance to explain that fight to myself, it wasn't until a few years later that I slowly decoded what exactly happened.

People thought I had become an angry girl, a sensitive one who just cries over every little thing. They would think my tears were shed for no reason. But, in my head, I kept telling them that they did not know what I knew.

I am not sure where my brother was the night of the fight. He is not in the picture I had in mind from then, but I remember that I started to think that I had to protect him from knowing the evil that was going on in the house.

❀

We were a happy family that everyone would envy. Caring parents and two lovely, healthy kids. I did not like to be the one who proves it wrong. Actually, I always wanted to make my father proud. He was a respectable man in the family and his line of family name was the most important thing.

My father is from the nomad tribes, the Qashghaei. He is the first generation of that tribe who settled in a city. He had studied his elementary school with other nomad kids in different winter and summer schools where the tribes would travel along with all their sheep and tents.

In those tribes, father is a big figure. Everyone is known by their father's name. The closer you are in line of the "khan" succession, the more respected you are. And I was always proud of him. I knew any shame to him would shame myself.

Now that I look back, I hate myself for all those feelings and what lingered years after. I blame myself for being more angry at my mother for her cheating than my father's. To be honest, I do not know whether what they did was a mistake anymore.

I remember the first time I talked about it was with my therapist in Switzerland. It took me so many years to accumulate the courage needed to speak out. And her reaction shook me. She said, "Well, it is not a horrible mistake." And I was like, well, you do not know about my background and the mindset I grew up with.

About my mother, I realized that she had an affair with someone; she had an extra phone hidden in her bag. It was always there and she would only use it when no one was around. I had caught her using it when she was in the room by herself. It was like I had realized there was something going on that she did not want anyone to know about, and I let her think I didn't notice it every single time. Just as we would pretend that my dad had stopped his affair with that relative girl while he obviously hadn't. It was like a public secret that had to remain so for a bigger benefit, the benefit of his honor and the family's dignity.

It was a spring afternoon I think. I was in the second grade. My mom had come back from work and was about to take a nap on the sofa in the living room. It was just me and her at home and I asked if I could buy an ice cream for myself. She said I could grab some money from her purse in their bedroom. I went to the room happily to take the money. The moment I was looking for her wallet in the purse, my hand touched the hidden phone. I just knew that was the time I finally understood what was going on.

The decision wasn't a tough one. I just took the phone and unlocked it. It was an old classic Nokia 0011, very easy to unlock. And there it was.

A long list of a chat with a man I want to name Ali here. A man who was not my father. A man that I did not know and had exchanged many love messages with my mother. I was frozen from shock. But I had to quickly leave for the ice cream. I couldn't let anyone know that I knew.

I left home, got my ice cream and went to days of silence. I do not remember what was going on in my eight-year old mind. But I remember I went silent for weeks. It was strange. I would disagree with anything that anyone would say without any reason.

The silence slowly changed to panic attacks any time I thought my mother picked up her purse. Or anytime I thought my father was somewhere else other than where he had told us. My parents would always find a way to justify the attacks. Justifications that I never resisted accepting. They would think it was because of my school test, my puberty years, my quarrels with my boyfriends, etcetera. I could never talk to them about it. Even thinking about disclosing the secret was suffocating.

So far I knew my mother had an affair with a man and all I knew about him was his name. And that my father had an affair with that distant relative girl that I loved as a kid.

It was at a wedding that finally Ali got a face. We had gone to Shiraz for that wedding and all of our relatives were coming to the town from across the country. We were staying at someone's house whom I did not know. My father had left us there and gone to buy something I guess. My brother was not around. It was me, my mother, the old hosting couple and a young man named Ali. I am not saying that I immediately recognized him, but it was not at all difficult to understand that he was the recipient of all my mother's love messages.

My mother and Ali had underestimated me. But I could see what was going on. And it was tough. I was around ten years old.

I was thinking of these details when I was preparing my long, colorful, traditional Qashqaei costume to wear for a recent wedding. I remembered getting ready for that wedding. I remembered what made the whole thing worse was that this man was married. And I remembered we had gone to his wedding. It was then that I realized why my mother was nervous that night. Why was she weeping after she got home from that wedding?

But now that I think of that afternoon, I think how naïve and inconsiderate Ali and my mother were. Ali was leaning back on a traditional cushion. Why should have Ali asked me if his wife was more beautiful than my mother? Why did they leave me in the living room and go to the bedroom together when the old host couple were away?

I knew what was going on. They either underestimated me or did not care if I would get it. But there is something I can in no way forget, the authentic smile on my mother's face. She was happy, clearly happy.

I was sure then that I had a secret to hide. I had to hide it from everyone. It did not matter that my brother was older than I was, I knew I had to protect him from knowing what I knew.

Khadijeh, 60, Isfahan, Somayeh's mother
As told to Somayeh

These are the pages of my memoir that your hands are turning. How can you just stand, watch and do nothing?

I used to sort of murmur this song at the carpet workshops, but later sang them loudly along with my friends when I could manage a 15-20 minute escape, when no one was around.

I would pretend that I wanted to go do some random things, like checking if others were ready to go fetch water, so other friends would come to one of our friends' who had a more relaxed family. We would sing and dance together. One of our friends knew the basics of playing 'tombak' and I was the singer. My friends would tell me to sing, they said I had a voice.

Googoosh was very famous and trendy those days. There was a line that I liked. It says: "There is a calling from behind the walls, walls of my heart. I know the voice…" But my friends did not like it. They wanted an upbeat song so they could dance to it.

I can't remember all the lines as I stopped singing after some points. I think because I could not sing at our own house and later I got married and I never had the time or spirit of singing. My dad was against music and of course dancing. He was so religious that the first thing my sister and I had to do in the morning as soon as getting up from the bed was wear our head scarves. Only the circle of the face could be shown, not a single strand of hair. He would frown at us and shout if our brothers could see our hair. It did not matter to him that brothers were 'mahram' (religiously close family members who women do not have to cover in front of).

It seemed as if being happy was *haram*—forbidden—in our house. We shouldn't even laugh out loud. My dad used to say that Satan would get happy if he heard the sound of laughter.

So, those ten or twenty minutes of escape were time to be happy and sing.

Besides that, we had two or three other days in a year to have the whole house for ourselves. It was the grape harvest season in summer when not only my father and brothers would go to the farm to harvest their fruits, but our mothers had to go with them to help so the grapes would not rot on trees.

It meant that all house chores were on us, daughters. But we would do all the work at home so fast, cleaning and preparing food for when they return, and then we had the rest of the day for ourselves.

❁

My friends would come to our house because we had a pond and we could go into the water and play.

So, that was the plan: on the first day we would quickly clean and wash the pond which would only be used for watering the garden and washing the dishes. Then we would drag water out of the well using the windlass. We would take turns to turn the wheel and carry the bucket and in about an hour the pond would be full and we would undress and go play in the water. We could happily scream and shout and sing and dance without anyone around to hear us. We then would quickly settle everything in its former place and my friends would go back home before people returned from the farms. Those were probably the happiest times of our childhood, when we would laugh loud and could hear our friends laugh.

There were few winter nights when we would go to our relatives' place to sit and spend the long nights. There was no television at the time. People knew nothing about politics those days, so no political discussions, no games, nothing. The only thing we would do was recite the Surah al-Hamd from the Quran and the rest of what we say in our daily prayers. The older people would correct the mistakes in our Arabic accent. Even in those rounds of prayer reciting sessions, girls would not talk. We would just sit and listen to the boys and fathers. My father would renounce anyone even having a smile on their faces at the time, saying it was disrespectful to Quran and prayer.

❖

I got married when I was 13. I had never seen my husband before we religiously became man and wife.

Here is how it started.

I remember that it was a weekend but I was at a carpet workshop, working. About two or three hours into work, my mother came and told me to go with her to my sister's place because a few of our neighbors had decided to go on a one-day trip and the driver wanted to do a headcount. I got extremely happy because I did not need to work on the weekend and for the first time I was hearing about going on a trip. I quickly grabbed my chador and went with her.

But we did not go to my sister's. Instead, we went to one of her neighbors. It was only us and the neighbor. Then came a man, who they told me was the driver. The neighbor brought us tea. I was waiting for the rest of the people who would join the trip. But the driver left after he had tea. And a few minutes later my mother said that we had to leave. I asked where the other people were, and why the driver did not wait to count everyone after they came. My mom just said that was it. I went back to the workshop and spent the rest of the weekend weaving.

A few days later, I would see my mother was setting up the home and cleaning everywhere as what we normally do for Norouz, to get ready for the rounds of relatives coming for a new year visit. I would also hear things, like some people were supposed to give us a visit and sit for writing "the contract." I thought they meant the buying and selling contract of some farm or land that sometimes my dad had with his farm mates.

Then came the day. I remember I had come back home from carpet weaving for the lunch break and was taking a short nap before leaving again. It was when my sister, Fatemeh, 15 years my senior, woke me up, saying, "Hey, you! Get up! Do you know it is all about you? We are marrying you off. We are going to send you out of the nest."

I remember the strange feeling in my stomach. I got up and quickly grabbed my chador and went to the carpet workshop. I told one of my mates there who was two or three years older than me. I told her what my sister had said. She soothed me saying this is what all of us had to do sooner or later.

Two of my friends from the carpet workshop, Batoul and Zahra, had gotten married before me. No matter how much the whole concept of marriage was shrouded in secrecy, it sounded like a duty to me. Everyone would do it, so I would accept it, too. It was up to my parents to decide. I was too shy to ask about any details like who the person is, or what I have to do. I had no one to ask. It was too much of a taboo for a girl to talk about.

Once my friend Batoul got married, she stopped doing carpet weaving. After a few weeks, I missed her so much and asked my mom if there was a way to see her. Even if she was living just a few alleyways from our house, I was not allowed to go there, I did not know why. But once, my mother helped me to quickly give her a visit, telling my dad that I was going to help her aunt who was living in the same alley that Batoul did. So I went there and said hello, had a quick chat over tea and in less than an hour I was back home.

When I told my other friend at the workshop that I had visited Batoul, she frowned at me with disgust. She asked if we have discussed what she does with her husband. She told me it was very inappropriate for a girl to visit a newly wedded woman. I did not understand her reasoning as I did not know what she was talking about but, having realized there might be something inappropriate about a possible conversation about men, I did not share that I had seen Batoul with others.

Then came the day that my in-laws-to-be came to our home for the first time. They were served with tea and fruit and then the men of the family wrote the 'marriage contract' and left. The contract would include my 'mehrieh,' the amount of money that my husband had to pay me if he wanted to divorce me. I did not know the amount. No one asked me anything.

It was just a day or two before that I realized they were the same family who lived on a familiar backstreet, that my brother was going to marry their daughter. It was a scary thing. I knew that it would never be easy. And then one of the women at the workshop told me, "You are doomed." She believed that when two families exchange bride and groom both families will be affected not just by their own troubles, but also by any problem that the other family goes through.

But my sister told me not to care about what they say. And later my mom said once I get married, I should never share what happens at my husband's house with others.

I was also worried because I had never heard anything good about the men of that family. That they were such angry men who would fight over any minor matter. I had heard that their daughters are not sincere at all. And, like everyone else those years, I knew that I had to live with them in a room at their house for years.

A few days after the contract signing, we had the religious ceremony of marriage. It was then that I realized that the supposed bus driver was the groom. At least he knew what the person he wanted to marry looked like.

I was extremely shy and could not look at his face. I would keep my face down not to look at him. I am sure he was the same. It was a strange feeling sitting beside a man who I did not know at all. I did not raise my head even when I wanted to put the gift watch my mom had bought for him around his wrist. Of course I did not look at him either before or after he put a necklace around my neck.

Mahsa

There are some moments in my life so dark that I am ashamed to remember them and talk about them even to myself. How on earth can anyone understand what you mean by "I attempted suicide for a pair of jeans?" Yet, it is what I did when I was 15.

After saving up for months I finally bought a pair of black jeans. I loved the blue ones but I knew my mom would never let me wear blue jeans. Here was my mom's rule: any light color or any piece of clothes that attract attention are forbidden for girls and women. So she had this monthly or weekly ritual of rummaging through my stuff to find anything that could possibly violate that rule, something like a pair of white socks. It turned out that according to my mom black jeans were an "eye catcher" too.

When I got home I went directly to my room (which actually was not "my room," we never had our own rooms; it was just a room that I shared with my younger sister and brother and often with guests). My mom came right after me, without asking any question, grabbed my shopping bag, took out the jeans, and said I should go to the shop the next day and give them back.

Then she went to our neighbor. That night I couldn't blink an eye, thinking, "I don't want to live anymore." It was not just the stupid jeans. Wearing something that I loved was never a dream that would come true in my whole life. Since I was a little girl I always felt ugly in the clothes that she permitted me to wear.

So the next day I found some mouse poison in the pantry, stirred it in a glass of water and drank it. I still remember the taste of it.

I had a friend named Farnaz who often came to our door; then we walked to school together. I still don't know in what condition my mom found me but that day my friend came, my mom let her in, so she absolutely knew what was happening. Farnaz took me to hospital and there they saved me and sent us home, without bothering to wonder why a 15 year old girl tried to kill herself

The saddest part—it still bothers me—was that my mom knew what I had done and did absolutely nothing. She never mentioned a word about it. If Farnaz hadn't come over that day, I doubt that my mom would've done anything at all to save me.

Now I am a 43 year old woman, and the mother of a 23 year old girl. It's been years of my mom trying to get emotionally connected with me but I just can't.

I don't have a single memory from my childhood of my mom hugging me. Actually the first time I felt that my mom loved me was when I was in the labor room giving birth to my child. The pain was gripping and loosening and I was shouting and crying. In a very short silence I heard my mom crying behind the door of the labor room. And at that specific moment I thought, "Oh, she loves me."

I spent the first 11 years of my childhood in Qom (the most religious city of Iran). All people that I had any contact with were religious, including our relatives, neighbors, people on the street. The first woman I saw in my life without a hijab was on the cover of a cookery book belonging to my mom. She was a blond, slim young woman wearing a short skirt (again, first short skirt I ever saw), she was holding a bowl and stirring something in it, maybe flour.

We were living in a narrow long house with all the rooms in a row, something like a boarding house. After the front door there was my father's study that served as a guest room too, just male guests. My two older brothers used to go out to play with their friends and ride bikes. As I was a girl, I was not allowed to go out.

I spent all my childhood by myself, painting or playing with toys. I particularly loved to spend time in my dad's study surrounded by books or in a small room that my mom used as a store room. I had some cousins that had a relative living in Usa. This guy used to bring barbies as a souvenir for my cousins. These barbies were not something to play with or even to touch; my cousins used to put them as decorative objects in shelves with glass doors, locked doors! They occasionally brought the dolls out and I was allowed to have a close look at them.

Now whenever I look at my daughter's Barbies I wonder if I was unconsciously buying them not for my child but for myself. When I was around seven, I had a beautiful dress with a pleated skirt that I loved, but when I wore it with a big scarf that covered my long hair I felt I was the ugliest girl in the world. Actually it was what I felt till I got married, when I no longer had to wear a full covering.

I feel ashamed when I think about my obsession with clothes all my life. It was not just about religion. Clothes, and appearance in general, was the last thing in the world my mom cared about. I saved my pocket money, sometimes stole some from my dad's wallet to buy some clothes. But it was never enough to feel good. Because, for example, I would buy a shirt but a nice shirt doesn't look nice when you wear it with worn pants and shoes.

Some days ago my friend and I were going to a party. As I was in my friend's place she offered me to choose one of her dresses. I picked an elegant green dress. Just before leaving I felt I was suffocating; I urged her to unzip the dress and went to the party with my casual clothes. Elegant dresses make me feel stupid. I feel I am trying to be someone that I am not and people would notice it.

My mom used to say that I am her punishment from God. I remember her praying: "Please God, guide this girl or kill her." She used the word "kill," not some less brutal expression like "take her." (My worst sins were that I didn't fully cover my hair). That's why I think the day I tried to commit suicide she probably hoped that… I don't know. It hurts even to think about it.

My mom lost both of her parents when she was five years old. One morning in winter, after a heavy snow, the roof of their house collapsed in front of her eyes. "After that," she said, "I was like a ball my relatives kicked to each other." Her relatives didn't let her go to school. Instead she was babysitting their children or doing their chores. She always says that she will never forgive them.

When I was in my last year of high school and studying for the university entrance exam, she kept telling me, "Don't bother, I will never let you go to universities, where boys and girls are sitting next to each other and God knows what they are doing."

I try to forgive my mom because I know what she has been through. I really try, but I just can't.

Marziyeh, 38, housewife

My childhood was both sad and happy. I was a daddy's girl. Unlike my mom, he always had my back. He would take me to the park, buy me junk foods I liked, and play with me. Actually, I was his favorite kid. But, when it comes to my mother, it is more of a sad story. She was the one who would tell my father not to take me with them on trips. They would leave me at my grandma's, but used to take my two other sisters with them, both older than me. It still stays with me as a complex when people talk about going on trips. It reminds me of being a broken hearted little kid seeing my parents going on trips with my two sisters, but not me.

However, I must say I had a good time staying with my grandma, my mother's mother. Like my father, she was also good at entertaining me, playing with me, etc.

My father used to take me to his workplace. He used to have a shop. But the good days all passed when my father went bankrupt and was left jobless. It was then he started using drugs.

I have gone through days that I never want my own kids to experience. I do whatever I can to keep them away from tasting the sadness and helplessness that I had to bear.

My school days were full of the most bitter days I remember. Not only were the days of going to the park with my dad over, we became very poor. I was always being humiliated because my classmates would laugh at me for my torn shoes or old clothes. I had to wear my older sisters' clothes. I would never have any snacks in my bag for the break times. I never liked school for those sad feelings.

I am 38 now, and still I wonder why my parents did not do more. Why didn't they take me on a trip with them? Why did my father not go to work after he went bankrupt? Did he not see us suffering? Why did my mother not make us breakfast for even one single day before we went to school? Why did they not care? Why did she not care?

I loved my dad, I still do, but he could've done more. He could look at his kids and their sufferings, stop using drugs and start doing some decent work.

And my mother, she could be kinder to us. She always recalls her own childhood filled with great memories, with great joy of going out and playing with her friends beside Zayandehrood River in Isfahan.

My mother was the first child of a well-off family. She says she was such a precious gift to her parents after seven years of their marriage. Her parents used to provide all the best for her, from recreational activities to booking the best doctors in Isfahan when she became sick. But she would not do the same for her own kids.

I think my parents could do much more for us. I remember my sister started to work as a cashier in a pharmacy when she was only 18. She would pay for all the household; that shows how we were raised.

Now, I can remember the nights we had nothing to eat. It was a recurrent thing back then that my mother used to pour water into a pot, put it on the stove and turn on the stove pretending she was cooking dinner. We would wait forever till she finished cooking and would finally fall asleep hungry. Now, I can also understand how tough it was for them.

My parents used to fight over everything. My mother would ask my father to get out of home and find a job; he would fight back with nonsense. And me and my three other sisters would go to the room until the fight was over. We would close the door and try not to get involved or we would be beaten. Then, when things would get slightly calmer, we would get out of our cave, trying to help them reconcile and assuring them that everything was going to be alright.

But, I expect my mother to do more now, at least.

She could come visit me after I gave birth to my child. But it was after a week she came only to stay for a few hours and leave for weeks after that. She never helped me after my delivery when I was in pain. Nor did she deal with how to raise my kids.

When I think of my parents and my childhood, I think I have to become better of a mother than my mom. I sit with my 3 year old daughter and talk to her when she is sad, when she cries, when she is upset. I talk to her. My mom never talked to us.

To be honest, after some point, I decided not to talk to her either. Because even if she talks to us, she keeps criticizing us and victimizing herself. She always blames me for whatever happens in my life.

Jila, my sister, has epilepsy. Every single time she goes through a seizure, my mother starts blaming her for not taking her medication, not eating proper food, or not getting enough rest. She does not show any empathy.

I used to talk to my father, though. He would listen. He would advise me what to do in my life, with my husband, about his job, etc. My dad would not hesitate to support me in what I would decide. For example, he stood by my side when I decided to wear a hijab after my marriage. Ali, my husband, asked me to wear a full hijab, chador, if we got married. I accepted. It was not a big deal to me. I remember everyone was in shock when they saw me wearing a long black veil. They used to ask me how I could change so dramatically.

I used to wear lots of makeup at work, I used to polish my nails constantly or wear very colorful clothes. Now, suddenly, I changed into this conservative outfit.

My mother did not disagree either. She told me to do whatever my husband says and wear clothes in any way that he wants. My dad wanted me to do the same.

I think I became a happier person after my marriage. My husband takes me on trips. He likes me and I like him. Of course we have fights over many things. Like his joblessness. But, what can I do? Whatever I say to him can trigger a fight. A fight that I do not want my children to witness. Because I have seen enough of them in my own childhood.

I have started to compromise. That is very needed in a shared life.

Whenever it comes to a point that my husband and I are about to start a fight I remain silent or I change the topic. I do not say anything. My whole body starts to shake. I know that if we start a fight, the first thing he would tell me is go to my parents' house. What can I do in such a situation? With such a mother at home?

All I do is take refuge in my mother-in-law. She has been kinder to me than my mom and my sisters. She always listens to me, talks to me. She tells me how we have to become more patient in life.

I do not mean that my husband is horrible. Last week, he surprised me with a birthday party. He had bought me a few good gifts. But you know what? I would like him to appreciate me and what I do in life. None of the gifts could make me happier than him quitting smoking at home where our little kids are.

Khadijeh

Those days people wouldn't like women to spend time out of home if they did not have a necessary thing to do. I used to go to our neighbors' places to weave carpets until I learnt it well. Then I got my own loom to weave at home.

It wasn't an easy job to convince carpet weavers to teach you how to read the design from the design map.

Our neighbor, Jamileh, had the carpet loom at her place. Others would go to her house to weave. She had five or six kids from newborn to about seven and was always overwhelmed by loads of chores. What I would do to convince her to teach me how to read the carpet design was to go there very early every morning much before others would come to weave. Then, I'd help her clean her house, give breakfast to the kids and clean the carpet loom. I loved carpet weaving so much that I would do anything to learn it.

It is how I managed to buy Jamileh's attention. She started to count on me more than others and finally agreed to teach me design and pattern reading.

I remember the day she wanted to teach me. It could not happen in front of other weavers. She told me that I had to pretend I wanted to stay longer to help her with the kids when everyone else was about to leave. Because, if they knew she wanted to teach me, they would want to learn, too.

I was surprised that it only took half an hour. I got the whole pattern reading in only half an hour, and then I was no longer dependent on others to read the pattern for me to weave.

I should also say that it wasn't just for being the apple polisher that I'd help Jamileh with her housework and cleaning the loom place. I liked to be in a neat, tidy place. And Jamileh was a nice person. She had a good heart. Sometimes when I wanted to go back home after work, she would tell me to ask my mother if I'd stay for lunch the day after because she was going to cook something special.

By special I don't mean that it was a very fancy meal like what we say these days. It would be like a stew with some meat in it. Those years people were all thin and skinny. We didn't have fat people. We wouldn't eat much and everything was so natural and organic. In the spring and summer it was the season of melon and watermelon; we used to eat watermelon and bread in the morning. In winter it would become some beans and wheat, boiled with some herbs as a sort of soup. We would have a cup of that with bread.

Unlike dinner, lunch was a meal we would rarely have together. My dad, my brother and their two workers—at that time they were called "bondmen"—used to have yogurt and bread every day. Four grown-up men would have less than a kilogram of yogurt for lunch for farm-working days as long as 14 hours. At home, lunch was not much fancier. For almost all of summer we used to have vinegar diluted with some water and mixed with some mint, and if we were lucky, some grated cucumber.

But dinner was when we would have the most proper meal and we would sit around each other talking about our days. I remember that rice was a sort of luxurious food to have those days. We would mostly have some soup or stew with meat two or three times a week.

The taste of the stews my mother used to make is still fresh in my mouth. She did not need to tell me how to make them. I would stand next to her looking at her way of cooking and learning it. It was not a big deal. It was like I was just doing my responsibility at home. But, still once I made a terrible mistake for making the simplest thing: eggs.

It was winter that my mom went to Tehran to visit her parents who lived there at the time, because my uncle used to work there at the time. I was nine or ten years old and my twin sister and brother were about three years old. Mom took Mohammad with her on the trip and left Batoul with me at home.

We used to have hens at home and used their eggs or exchanged them with neighbors for what we needed. But my mother asked me to make sure I would make the eggs for ourselves so she was sure we would get enough food in her absence.

There was no gas at homes, neither gas pipes nor gas cylinders. Oil was rarely used. We'd use wood to make fire to bake bread and warm the house. But it would be very smoky and it was tough to have so much wood every day, so we had to mix the wood with cow dung to curb the smoke and slow down the burning. There were special big buckets that we had for mixing and putting this organic fuel in. To warm the room, we would put the bucket under 'corsi,' a low-height table made with thick sticks covered by a huge heavy quilt. In all houses it was the only warm spot in a cold winter, where you could sit around it on the floor and cover yourself with the nicely warmed quilt from toes to shoulders.

❖

I remember that some days in the morning my mom would place the pot of food ingredients into the bucket under the corsi so it was cooked slowly for dinner.

So, when mom was away in Tehran, I followed her way of cooking and placed two eggs into the mix of wood and dung before I took my sister to the public bath for our weekly wash.

When we came back, a disgusting smell had dominated the whole house. The eggs had exploded inside the corsi. My sister was about to throw up. I quickly grabbed a piece of cloth and took the bucket out of the corsi and dug a hole in the garden and covered the whole mess there. Of course not the bucket itself. I washed the bucket so the smell went away. My friends later told me I was smart. I did that just in time so my dad would not notice the mess when he returned from the farm.

Even if my dad did not notice the mess and my mom was not around, I felt very guilty inside for not being able to make the eggs. Then, I decided to make it up. What I did was that instead of making two or three eggs every day for myself and my sister, I would make only one or some days none. What I did though was put some straw in a basket and save other eggs I had. Until the day my mother came back, the basket was beautifully full of eggs. She was happy seeing I had gathered them so neatly. I put the burden of guilt off my shoulders.

Things that I would hide from my mother were mostly on this scale. One other thing that I managed not to tell her was how I started to wash my hair with powder detergent. They were also a new thing when I was nine or ten. For washing the body and clothes, we only had homemade soaps which were of very low quality. They were so greasy. It did not matter how much I would wash my very thick hair, it was still dull, fuzzy and frayed making it tough to comb.

Once I was complaining to a neighbor about my thick hair saying I wish I'd lose some of it. She told me she'd heard that if we wash our hair with powder detergent, then it would cause hair loss. It was an amazing hint. But I knew that my mom would be mad at me if she realized I wanted to lose my hair, because having thick long hair was a big beauty criteria. So, I started to smuggle some powder to the public bathroom with me.

The difference between these detergents and the thick greasy soaps was that they would wash my hair to a shiny look. I would even hide it from my girlfriends in the public bathroom, because I was afraid they might mention it to my mom just randomly. But it didn't remain a secret for long.

Since I started to wash my hair with the detergent, my friends' mothers noticed that their daughters' hair was not as shiny as mine when we were back from the hamam. In the beginning they kept criticizing their daughters that they would not wash their hair thoroughly enough and made me an example of a neat, clean girl who doesn't just play around the hammam and would focus on washing herself and getting clean. After a few times, however, everybody realized that was not the case. My friends started to ask me what I was doing with my hair because no matter how thoroughly they washed their hair with soap it wasn't like mine.

At the end I told them about my little secret, making them promise not to tell my mom. And, I have to add, the detergent never resulted in hair loss for me.

I loved the hammam ceremony a lot. It was a lot of fun for us, like the water fetching. We were all girls playing and sometimes singing in the hammam, telling jokes, talking about our days and eavesdropping on women who were talking about their own days, things that we normally wouldn't hear. Sometimes we would hear them consulting each other about finding wives for their sons. They would say things like, "Have you seen Asghar's daughter when she fetches water? She is so strong carrying two big jars of water and walking so swiftly." It was also where women could see all of the girls that they had considered for their sons, to make sure they are healthy or have a good body.

It was the water fetching, washing clothes at the pond, our time in hammam and mosques and carpet weaving when we had fun with our friends, and our families would feel safe that we were by ourselves. But sometimes there were precautions even in these places. Not all girls were equally trustworthy to our parents.

For example, those days when I was about to learn carpet pattern reading, there was a girl in the workshop, her name was Maryam. She was a few years older than me. I remember that once she did not come to weave and then she did not come the day after, and we heard that she was lost and had not gone home. She was lost for three or four days and people started to talk about her a lot. Everyone would say something. Some people said she was kidnapped, some would say she was killed and there were whispers that she had eloped with a boy. It was a big shock in the neighborhood.

Finally, she was found and her father beat her really badly. He wouldn't let her leave home anymore.

My mother wasn't afraid of me doing anything like her because she trusted me and knew I was so careful. But still she told me several times never to think about doing something like what Maryam did. She told me: "Look how everyone mocks her dad now. Look how her family is disgraced and ashamed in the whole town. Promise you would never follow anything that she has probably told you."

After a few weeks of her isolation, Maryam's mother came to the carpet workshop and asked Jamileh's husband for help and intervention. She said that her husband doesn't allow her daughter to do anything. Jamileh's husband was of those men who people would go to for reconciliation. And in this case, he could also help convince Mayram's father to let her back to the carpet workshop as it was a safe place with no men around.

Maryam came back and resumed working there. But things were not the same as when she had left. Women would look at her differently now and she had become very sensitive, reacting to any single thing. The atmosphere had become thick and heavy at the workshop and, after a while, Jamileh asked her not to come anymore.

I do not know what Maryam did after that, but I know that she got married to a guy from Isfahan, not in Dolatabad, our own town. People said no one from town proposed to her. But, now, after years, we occasionally see each other and talk about our lives and our memories at the carpet workshop. Last time she told me about her son getting married and that she sang one of the songs we used to whisper at the carpet looms.

I loved those songs, I initially learnt them by listening to the radio that my brother had bought. It wasn't a rare thing, but because it would play music, my father and almost all men in town did not allow us to listen to it. When I finally set up my own carpet loom at home, I would sometimes steal my brother's radio when he and my dad were away at the farm and would listen to it with a low volume while weaving my carpet.

I used to keep the volume low so I could hear my dad's bicycle when he'd enter the house and I could quickly turn it off.

One day, I remember I was singing along with "Aqasi," whose music was very popular those days, when I suddenly noticed my dad entering the room. I got so scared that I couldn't find the on/off button. I wanted to mute the radio but instead I turned the volume to the loudest. There was no more time, so I just left the room and tried to run away from him.

The poor man had an inherent problem with his leg. He wouldn't use a cane but limped heavily as he moved. He took the long broom that we used for the yard and chased me, shouting how dare I listen to the music in his house. At the same time he started to feel sinful because he himself was hearing it while chasing me. So, he left me and went back into the room to turn the radio off, but he didn't know how. He came back to the yard desperately and told me he'd promise not to beat me but I had to turn the radio off, quickly. I went back to the room carefully and ready to escape again if he wanted to beat me. I knew he wouldn't, but I wasn't sure. I forgot all the fear the moment I saw what my dad had done to the radio. He had thrown lots of blankets and pillows and buried the radio underneath to suffocate the volume. I couldn't stop laughing, but I had to as my dad came in. Seeing me laughing could make him even angrier.

It was the last time I listened to the radio for years. Not because I was afraid of being beaten, but because when my dad calmed down, he told me that listening to the music was haram and if I'd listen, then in the other world, flames of fire would go out of my ears because God doesn't want us to listen to music. I stopped listening because at the end of the day I thought it was not worth the risk, neither with God, nor with my dad.

Raha, 35

I was born in Qom (the most conservative city of the country). It was wartime (Iran and Iraq war). The first image I remember from my childhood is from when I was about two and we were sitting in the living room in front of the TV. I clearly remember a framed photo of Khomeini hanging on the wall on the top of the TV. In fact, the frame is the only clear thing I can recall from that moment, the rest are all vague and cloudy in my mind.

Next is what I remember from the day dad was coming back from the front. Maybe I was three. Baba came walking with a cane. I had missed him very much. I remember once getting stuck in the bathroom and would not leave, insisting that only Dad had to come and help me out.

It is sad that I do not have a single memory of my mother. Only that she would sleep at noon times and would force us to sleep, too. As I look back, I have no memories of my mother kissing or hugging me. Surely she had done that, but I do not remember anything.

I was four when we left Qom for Khorramabad. I loved to play with kids on the street but mom would not allow it. My brother, two years younger than me, and I would talk to children from behind the window.

Once I was about five, I went out around sunset time with a skirt, instead of wearing pants. Mom came and dragged me back home and hit me hard with the stick and piece of hose. She bruised me badly.

I loved being in the crowd. I would play clowns for the kids next door. I'd enjoy it deeply when I could make them laugh. I think we were supervised by strict and stupid adults. Despite their severe control over us about what to wear or how to behave, they didn't seem to care much for us. Once we had a group of guests at home. While adults were having lunch in the living room, we children were in the bedroom. I remember one of the children pulled down my pants and his. I was choking with fear, but I was also too afraid to say anything to anyone. Or I remember the neighborhood kids touching me a few times when we were at the age of sexual curiosity. I still feel like throwing up when I remember that. Our parents seemed too busy that they could not care about these incidents; maybe because they had too many children that they could not oversee all of us.

I'd love to go to religious chanting ceremonies along with mom. To me it was a fun recreational thing to do as I would play with other girls and have sweets together. I remember once I wore a pair of long, black women's socks to join mom in her religious meetings and my sister mocked me for wearing them because she found it to be very ugly. But I did it anyway.

Mom was pathologically obsessed about religious purity. If I would fall while playing and my leg would bleed, it was not the pain that would bother me but the thought that my mom would start many rounds of washing me so I would not bring the impurity of blood into our home.

Every time we went shopping with Mom, she would do lots of bargaining with the shopkeepers and almost always we would leave the shop without buying anything. Once there was a pair of shoes that I loved badly, but mom did not buy them and instead got me another pair that I never liked. I hated them. I still remember their shape.

I used to be terribly afraid of hell, as mom would describe the tortures there with detail. She would tell me how I could be hanged by my hair in hell if I showed it in public. I always had this question in mind: "Why should I be hanged?"

I don't remember my mom giving me any feeling of love and affection.

It was my brother who took me with him to register me at school. First we went to a relatively good school; they had an entrance test on a very primitive level, with questions about names of colors. But I didn't even know green and blue. So he registered me at another school.

On the first day, my mom and dad took me to school and told me to come back with the school bus, but I took the wrong bus. I did not know I could ask help from anyone from school. So I just started walking. It was a kind of exploring and discovering the city by myself. One of our relatives accidentally saw me in front of a window shop and asked what I was doing there. Then she took me home.

I loved going to school. I did not do kindergarten and I loved being with people in a group. I was a very careless child and always lost my books and stuff. I was great in math but terrible with dictation and spelling. Mom did not hit me or confront me in any way when she saw my report card, but I remember the way she looked at me which made me feel very ashamed of myself.

I failed in my dictation class and I had to go to school for a makeup summer course. Other students would laugh at us on the street pointing at us, calling us "lazy and dumpy" children. I later realized that many people have problems with writing. A problem that has something to do with a part of the brain.

I hated writing. It would hurt my hand. I'd become stressed. I always wished I had a typewriter machine that would write my homework. One day I told one of my classmates about it. She told me that she had a typewriter that would write all of her homework. I asked her if she could use it to write mine, too. But she said her machine would only write hers. It was from her that I learnt I could also bluff.

It was when I started telling lies, like we used to be very rich before my dad went bankrupt, or that we used to have sofa and armchairs at home but we'd sold them, while in reality we never had any until I finished college.

No one at home would ever ask me if I had homework to do or what I should do for school. I used to feel my heartbeats every single time my teacher wanted to check our homework. I still get stressed when I remember it. Once I was kicked out of school early because I hadn't done my homework. When I got home no one asked why I was back so early. But I loved school anyway.

The first time I talked to a stranger boy was the day I sneaked out of the class and left school exactly when the teacher wanted to check the homework. I went back home. But this time I knew I should not get home before I was expected. So I wandered around the nearby park. Those days it was illegal to have a VHS player at home, but one of our neighbors had one and their children used to tell us the stories of movies they'd watched. I remember I told that stranger boy about one of the films of Jackie Chan, pretending that I had watched it myself. His jaw dropped when I told him the details of beheading someone with a guillotine.

I remember my older brother would tell stories to my little brother and me at night. I loved that. I wanted to be like my sister. She was my role model. She was the center of attention in the family; everyone admired her. When I learnt that my teacher had a son named Mehran (which sounded like an elegant name to me) I wished my sister would marry him.

One day my sister was recording my younger brother's voice. I said, "Please record my voice too." I wasn't jealous of my brother at all, but when we were teenagers he was a real pain in the ass. He was very naughty and always got on my nerves. And everyone told me that you are older than him, you should behave better. One day I got really angry and said, "For God's sake I am just two years older than him. Why am I the one who should be a good guy? Why does nobody say anything to him?"

In my daydreams I had a few handsome brothers. They had a Nissan Patrol and drove me around. They took me to playgrounds. They were very supportive. In those dreams, there was no such thing as a hijab. At weddings or religious ceremonies women and men were not separated. Women wore no hijab. My parents were not in my dreams. Don't know why.

When I was around ten, one day on my way back home from school, I stuffed my chador in my bag. My mom saw me in the alley and gave me a lesson I never forgot. She beat me badly.

Later, when I was older and whenever I was out and my hair was not fully covered, if I saw a woman in a hijab I felt uneasy. I felt the weight of my mom's hard look, as if that woman would judge me.

When I was at middle school one day my mom was on a trip and I cooked for the first time. Since then I started to do chores at home. Maybe as a way to be noticed. Nobody forced me to do that. But I liked being admired. I liked when others said, "Oh poor thing. You did that all on your own?"

I don't remember being encouraged before that, maybe just for reciting the Quran, or little money that my dad gave me as a reward when I passed my final exams with good marks.

My pocket money was next to nothing. Mostly I took food from home to eat at school.

I liked some kind of cookie that cost more than the money I had. Sometimes I stole money from my dad's pocket to buy my favorite cookie.

Khadijeh

I was born in Dolatabad. I don't know what year or what day. My parents did not get me a birth certificate or an ID. They just decided to give me the ID of my sister who had recently died. Her name was Roghayeh. This is why my name on my ID is Roghayeh but everyone calls me Khadijeh. Roghayeh had died after falling into the small pond we had at home. She might have been trying to wash something in that little pond. And drowned in the water with no one noticing.

Our house was big and old. It had a big yard with two rooms far from the pond. The yard was almost vacant. There was that pond and a garden of 40 sq meters in the middle. My father used to plant some vegetables and herbs there that we would use for cooking. Things like mint and radish. And there was a well, too. People used to have wells at their houses as there was no water pipe or tap water. We'd use the well water for washing and watering the garden. My dad had made that well. Then we would take water up using rope and a bucket. But for drinking water we had to go to the village spring. It was around a 10-15 minute walk.

We would take big jars and go to the spring that was called "Khoshi Spring" because it was in the Khoshi neighborhood. We had to go either very early in the morning or late at night when the water was clean. Because some people would use that water for washing clothes, too. Maybe those who did not have a well at home.

I started to fetch water when I was around five. It is one of my favorite chores to do, as I could leave home. And I could hang with other girls in the alley. We were five or six girls more or less the same age. The first year we would go on foot. But, later on, we sometimes would ride the donkey we had, to fill and carry the big water jars. My dad would not allow me to go with the girls. So, when he wasn't home I would seize the chance to join them. He would allow me to go to the spring with my mother though. But still, my mom would send me with the girls when my dad wasn't around, when he was away on the farm.

It was a fun walk or ride to the spring with the girls. We would play on the way. Sometimes we would stop to pick some herb named tragopogon which we couldn't find in our own neighborhood. We would eat some and take the rest home to share with others. Or we would take lots of silverberries and eat on the way and throw them at each other.

Even if we would go early in the morning, still we could see women washing clothes in the spring. So we would keep going to reach upstream, that had the cleanest water. We wouldn't boil the water. We would just drink that or make food with it right away.

One of my sisters was killed bringing water. I was very little. I can't recall it myself. As my mom told me, I should have been around a year old when it happened. That day, my brother and two of my sisters had gone to Khoshi Spring to bring water. They had been around the place where women would wash their clothes. That's where the remains of a wall of a very old building collapsed and fell over people around the spring. Shahrbanoo, one of my sisters, died right at the scene and my oldest sister, Fatemeh, was injured at her feet. In the beginning my parents were worried thinking my brother had also been killed because he had gone with my sisters to help them. That is how it used to work. It was not appropriate to let girls go out alone for whatever reason. It should be either with mothers, brothers, or a custodian.

But fortunately, that day, my brother Hossein had left his sisters on the way to go play with his friends and had not been around the spring when the wall had collapsed on his sisters. My mother used to tell us how happy they were when they realized he wasn't injured.

(Right now, as I am writing this, both Fatemeh, who was injured at the wall, and my uncle, who had gone playing, are dead. My uncle died of cancer three years ago when I was still in the U.S. and my aunt just two days ago due to COVID. It is strange to write about them now...)

It is strange that I lost two sisters, Roghayeh and Shahrbanoo, for reasons related to water. I got my ID from the first one and have no memory of the second one.

I want to talk about my sister Fatemeh, but I will get back to it. First I want to tell you about our neighborhood custodian that I mentioned.

In our neighborhood that person was a woman named Robabeh. So, when I told you I used to go fetch water with my friends, we could never go by ourselves. It was either I would go with my mother, or if it was with friends, we had to coordinate it with Robabeh. We could go only if she wanted to bring water. Then we were allowed to join her in bringing water. She was such a stubborn woman. I do not know who had given her this position. But it was like everyone had agreed that she was responsible for the chastity of the girls in the neighborhood. Our mothers would agree and welcome that interference because they were so busy with so many kids they had and would appreciate an extra hand to help them control their girls outside of home.

Sometimes we sit with my friends from those days and talk about how we hate her now more than when we were kids. She was the one who persuaded our dads not to let us go to school.

Even in those years, there was a school that girls could go to. But Robabeh has told our already religious fathers that it is not appropriate for girls to go to school. I remember that my dad would tell us, "It is religiously forbidden that a woman puts pen on paper."

Besides a formal school in the village, there was a woman who would teach the alphabet and reading and writing to girls at home. My mother took me there secretly, without my dad knowing. I was in the clouds. But when my dad realized, he got angry and threatened my mom not to do that again. Even if I tried to learn reading and writing years later, after the Islamic Revolution in what they called "the literacy jihad" (a program to teach reading and writing to adults), I could never learn it. By then I had already been so occupied with my husband, three or four kids and housework, that I did not have the time or focus to learn. It has always remained a lifelong dream for me.

I do not know why Robabeh would do that. She herself was a strong woman at the time. She had several kids, all grown up and already married. She used to work at the farm by herself. She was sort of independent. Still she was against the girls' schooling.

It was not the only thing she was responsible for. We still talk about her as the "patrol of the neighborhood." She was the one that people would refer to for asking advice on anything, from finding a wife for their son to getting information on what is a good piece of farm land to buy. I never knew who had given her that title or how she managed to get that power. But that was a kind of rule, that if Robabeh was against us going to school, then it was not a choice anymore.

She would help women in the neighborhood, too. For example, when my own mother gave birth to her twins, my sister Batul and my brother Mohammad, Robabeh would help her take care of them when she was busy baking bread or helping my dad with his farm work.

I learned carpet weaving when I was six at my friend's house, Batul. Her father was one of the first people who started the carpet business in Dolatabad. Before that, women would do more canvas weaving. That was easy and cheap. But carpets were more complex and they would pay more. Besides, I loved to hang out with girls in the neighborhood because I did not have a sister at home and my mother was always busy. And my older sister was already married when I was two or three. So, I embraced learning carpet because I could spend time with my friends at the carpet loom.

I remember the first time I got paid for my work. After two months of weaving, I had mastered all of the skills, from different ties to reading patterns, scissoring and refining the ties. I remember I got 20 tomans for the first two months. When I got home I gave the money to my mother.

"Do you want a pair of earrings?" my mother asked. I got so happy and agreed. She took me to the jewelry shop and I chose a pair of earrings which had become fashionable at the time. All my friends had them. They were called "Ashrafi model." I remember they cost 18 tomans. Considering the size of the earrings as I remember, they would surely cost as much as a professional employee's monthly wage these days.

My mother never hesitated to let me spend the money I had made for myself. She did not ask me to spend the money at home for the daily expenses. My father did not say anything about how I had spent the money for myself.

I never had gold earrings before then, or any earrings I can recall, except for a pair that are actually the first memory I have from my childhood. I remember nothing from my life before that moment.

I should have been two or three years old. I remember that I was sitting on my sister's fiancé's lap. His name was Abbas Ali. He was putting on me a pair of small earrings with a dark blue gem that had a woman's face engraved on them. All I recall is that I was very shy but very excited that as soon as he put that in my ear I ran to my mother to show my earrings. I think my mother told me they were his souvenir he had brought me from his pilgrimage to Mashhad (holy city in the northeast of Iran, where the 8th Imam of Shia Muslim is buried).

My sister, Fatemeh, who had survived the wall collapse, might have been 16 when she got married to Abbas Ali. They were already engaged when the wall fell on my sister. Abbas Ali had told my mother that many people had asked him to divorce Fatemeh as she was "broken" after she had broken her leg in that incident. My mother always remained thankful to Abbas Ali because he did not divorce my sister. It could mean that she had become a divorcee at her father's home forever.

I can't recall Fatemeh and Abbas Ali's wedding. I should have been very little, maybe three or four years old. And my sister should have gotten married at around 19; that was too old for girls to get married at the time.

❖

My sister had three or four miscarriages before her first child, Morteza, was born; I was around seven or eight years old. Knowing all techniques needed to weave Isfahan carpets by then, I had become a professional carpet weaver and I stopped going to my friend Batul's place for weaving. Instead, my mother sent me to my sister's so I could teach her how to weave and it could keep her busy during the day. I would go from around eight in the morning to four or five in the evening. One or two years after that, I got my own carpet loom at home.

But one of my best memories from those years is of when my first nephew was born. As a tradition in the village and despite all restrictions of women moving around or spending time out of home, when a woman would give birth to her child, it was the responsibility of the grandmother—from mother's side—to take care of the newborn the first ten days.

Especially in my sister's case, as she had those miscarriages, my mother stayed with her for that time. When my mother was there, I was responsible for the housework and taking care of my dad and my brothers when they would come back home from the farm. But one of those ten days, when my father was away at the farm, I sneaked out of the house and went to my sister's to visit her and the newborn.

I clearly remember how excited I was when I got to see Morteza. It meant a lot to everyone that my sister finally gave birth and the baby was alive and he was a boy and they had many visitors. Those days, people would cater visitors to the newborn boys with special delights made of almond with a sweet wrap. I remember they smelled like rose water. Abbas Ali gave me one and later when he realized I liked them, he gave me two more.

It was the first time I'd seen bananas in my life. I had never seen them before. I remember my mother asked Abbas Ali what they were, and he responded they are the fruits people would say are good for my sister as she was weak after giving birth. To me they looked like strange tree branches.

Abbas Ali wanted to give me one of them, but my mother did not let him, saying I did not know what they are and how they taste, so better not to waste them on me and save them for Fatemeh. Actually that was when he gave me more delight.

I was there for an hour or two and my mother asked me to leave and go back home so I'd be there when my father and brother would come home. It could make my dad angry if he had realized I had left home without his permission. But the problem was that he would not give me the permission anyway.

He was tough on us about anything outdoors, but he would help us with housework. He was not the kind of man to sit waiting for me to serve him when mom was not around. Even if he was tired after farming, he would make tea himself or help with the dishes.

My girlfriends from the alley and I would always dream of going out of home. The only times we were allowed to go out aside from water fetching or carpet weaving was three nights in Ramadan, the Qadr Nights. And what we would do was go to the nearby mosque. It was of the very few chances we could see girls from other neighborhoods as that mosque was where many would like to perform their special Ramadan ceremony.

(One of the memories I have from that mosque is about a speech a clergyman was giving. He was talking about the difference between a Muslim and a true believer. He said that the Pharaoh was a true believer in God. Because he himself knew that he was not the God, even if he would tell people he was and would ask people to worship him or do sacrifices for him. The clergyman was saying it is not enough to simply say that God is one and Muhammad is the prophet, but what matters most is that we find the truth in our hearts. I think I was around 11 or 12 at the time I heard this speech.)

We would leave Dolatabad just twice a year. Once with my family to visit my oldest uncle every new year who used to live in Isfahan (about

15 minute drive to the north of Dolatabad). And once a year there was a one-day pilgrimage to a holy shrine in Narmi (a small village close to Dolatabad, about a 30-40 minute walk).

❀

I would die for the day that we would go to Isfahan. The only chance I could get to see beautiful streets and shops. I remember my dad would tell us, "You are allowed to watch the shops as you are following me." Now I think about it and laugh that we were so thankful of him allowing us to do window-shopping and making us feel like he was doing us a favor.

And the other time we would leave Dolatabad was when Robabeh would take the girls of the alley to the holy shrine. We loved that. It was such an amazing hike that even the constant naggings of Robabeh could not kill the joy of it. She would tell us to not laugh out loud even if no one was around on the road except for us. We would lower our voices for a few minutes and would resume our own jokes and playful walks right after.

I remember there was a river on the way that we would pass over and rest a bit near the bridge that crossed it. It was beautiful scenery. These days, when my sons Mahdi or Hossein drive me to the shrine, I remember our laughs passing the bridge. The river has gone dry. Robabeh is gone. Most of our naughty girls band is now aged and sick. But the memory of the joyful laughs of girls wrapped in the veil has prevailed.

Mahsa

I told my mom that I was writing or trying to write something, and I wanted to talk to her. "It's a kind of interview, about you, about me, about us."

"Okay. Feel free. Call me whenever you have time."

The next day she called and said that she had already written her memories and would send them to me. She asked me if I can find a way to publish them, or maybe I can write a screenplay based on them. "Or it can be a series! There are a lot."

When I receive the mail, my hands start to shake. It is a heavy package, five notebooks, each one 100 pages, blackened by her sloppy handwriting, front and back of every single page. But it is not the weight of notebooks; it is the weight of her stories that shakes my hands.

I start to read:

At dawn, my mother woke me up. She poured some boiling water in a pot and said, "Take your sister to the yard. Wash your hands and then come back for breakfast." Last night she had dyed our hands with Henna. My baby sister was three years old. I was five. When we were out in the yard, before going to pee, I asked my sister to wait for me. But she said that she had some secret to share with mom and didn't want me to know it, so she went back inside. It was a two story house. We lived upstairs; downstairs was a byre where we kept our cows. When I was in the water closet, which was quite far from the main building, I heard a deafening voice of our neighbor, an old woman, screaming, "My God! My God!" I came out and saw that the stair was blocked by a heap of rubbles.

"What happened?" I asked the old woman.

"Nothing, nothing," she said as she asked another neighbor. "Take her out of here!"

People were gathering around the ruins which only five minutes ago was my home.

"I want to go to my dad! I want to see my sister! I want my mom!"

"For God's sake, someone takes this poor child out!"

My father's cousin and her husband adopted me. They had no children. They treated me with a lot of love and kindness. But people started talking. They started spreading nasty rumors: her foster dad will finally marry her! I was five and he was 45. He was one of the nicest people God has ever created. After a year they adopted another child and my father's cousin's behavior changed. She worked from 7 mornings to 13. I became the babysitter of the new child. In the afternoons I wasn't allowed to go out to play with the children of the neighborhood. She started to beat me whenever I went out.

There are five pages in the first notebook about this woman. About how angry she was and how she used to shout at my mom, how she beat her. This woman passed away 10 years ago at the age of 75. When I was young she was always very kind to us. I remember when my mom was hospitalized for some surgery; she came and stayed with us (we were five children). I want to call my mom and ask her why? Why after so many years she still talks ill of that poor woman who now probably is nothing more than a bunch of bones in her grave? I want to tell my mom that maybe that woman didn't know better too. But I don't. Because I know what she has been through, I know that very well, maybe too well.

So maybe I should tell her, "Do you forgive me for not forgiving you?" 🏵️

Mahsa Afaridah is the pen name of an author living in Tehran whose confidentiality we want to ensure given the current political situation in Iran.

FORGIVENESS: A TALK WITH THE AUTHORS

Mahsa Afarideh
Somayeh Malekian
Selin Thomas

Somayeh Malekian: You don't want to believe that you have to leave. I started getting warnings from the intelligence people, directions from the press office that you need to cover this story that way, you should stop doing it the other way, and stupid requests that you keep receiving and ignoring until you realize that they—by "they" I mean the intelligence and the official press office of the government—don't like you anymore. And then it's time to slow down, "OK," to avoid sensitive topics.

But at some point I started to get accusations, nothing documented, but verbal accusations that you realize have a meaning—it's a message—saying that if you continue you are no longer safe. So at that point, I told my editor at my media that these are the signals I'm getting, and based on my experience and knowledge of the situation it means…'blah blah blah.' We were working on that until suddenly my credentials were revoked and I got more serious and severe threats. Then I realized that some of my friends were under arrest, or they had been summoned to court, and they (my editors) realized that the threat was serious and I had to do something.

So I just left the country, came to Turkey to be safe and gave myself some time to realize what I want to do and what's best. So the idea of writing about our mothers and ourselves was one of a thousand thoughts that crossed my mind when I was here. And out of so many ideas, I stuck to that, and talked with Mahsa and we stuck to that together.

Selin Thomas: How did you know one another?

Mahsa Afarideh: We had a friend, we met, and little by little we got closer. I think it's been more than 10 years now.

ST: You met in Tehran?

MA: Yes

ST: And that's where you are now, Mahsa?

MA: Yes

ST: Are you conducting interviews in person now?

MA: No, I am doing all interviews by phone also—except for the part my mom sent me with a lot of her notes.

ST: What benefits are there to conducting these interviews by phone, and what disadvantages do you feel?

MA: Actually for me it has been difficult, apart from working with Somayeh which is always something that I enjoy: sharing our ideas, talking about the work. But in the interviews, when you go deeper and deeper into a lot of things that I've been trying to forget for so many years, it's like a therapy session. Maybe the benefit will show up later.

ST: How about you Somayeh?

SM: Partly, I think as a journalist I'm used to doing long interviews on the phone. But this is different because it has this essence of being so intimate and normally in those situations—talking to a friend, or your mother, or someone you care for—when they want to talk about memories that are touching, you normally would hold hands or, I don't know, offer a glass of water, just like what Mahsa said, as in a therapy session.

But we are in COVID as well; the COVID situation always imposes its own consequences, and in that way people have gotten used to these sorts of relations, even if it's tense, it's very personal and intimate. We are all familiar now with phone calls and they somehow can be even more helpful than being in the presence of someone because…it gives some sort of safe distance. The person can just hang up at any moment and, for me, the fact that they kept talking I like to interpret as a sign that they like to share what they are sharing.

ST: That's so interesting, especially the idea that distance can bring people closer sometimes. What is unique about mother-daughter dynamics in Iran? What is it to be a mother in Iran? What is it to be a daughter in Iran? And, this is a big question, but what does it mean to be a woman in Iran?

MA: What I'm saying may not be unique to Iranian women, but maybe we feel it more than other women in our daily life. Going out shopping, or to school, university, or work; every single moment of that is challenging. The story of marriage—when you want to get married, when you want to get divorced, for example—it's a whole system that is against you. It's not just some bad guy at your office, I don't know, or your brother or your father or your mom. You are standing in front of a whole system.

ST: How do you carve out an independent identity?

MA: That's a very interesting question because my thesis was about the identity of women and I read a lot about the elements that build someone's identity: the history, culture, family, society, everything. At the same time, I think identity is never something independent. You try to have some sort of independence, but you can never be detached from all the things that have a role in building your identity.

ST: Is this project both of your attempts to have agency in that identity, that you can't detach from? You are, it seems to me, attempting to understand it, to provide yourselves with a path forward.

MA: Yes, exactly. I think my whole life, my adulthood, it has been an issue for me to be someone I want to be. But like I said, it's an everyday fight, fight with your ideas, fight with what they are trying to teach you, with what they are trying to impose on you.

SM: May I add something here—about if writing these stories can give us agency. To me, narrating is a way of saying things differently. I think about something in my mind and when I start telling it to someone else or put it in writing, I start to say it differently. And about these women, me and Mahsa included, by telling them to just imagine every reader, the audience, I can reshape the dynamic by telling it.

It has happened so many times in my therapy sessions, in my diary writings or whatever, that I say something, I read something over and over and I realize that the whole meaning has changed in front of my eyes. There have been things that I never noticed before.

ST: Like what?

SM: Like there have been moments in my life—I'm not saying so many moments but there have been moments—that I would guess that something my mother was doing was out of jealousy. It was shocking because I would never expect my mother to be jealous of who I am or what I do or whatever I enjoy in life. But when I started to have these very, very long conversations, I could understand my mother better. I could understand where those feelings are coming from.

I'm not saying that those feelings are not jealousy, I'm not saying that I was getting it totally wrong, but I can say that I understand my mother in those specific moments better now because I listened more thoroughly, more carefully, and I thought about it over and over, not just by a single observation. Not that I was totally naïve before, but writing about it, talking about it, kind of cleared my mind in some ways.

ST: What is that impulse that we share? What is the impulse that you are working on? Why strain to understand your mothers?

SM: Moving on without understanding is just ignoring something, skipping it. But if I really want to move on—indeed, deeply—I need to feel it. I always tell my friends that people understand any sort of misery, any issue about health, or being poor, just to the level that they have experienced it themselves. Someone who has never been hungry can never understand what a hungry person really feels. Someone who has never been unable to move freely can never understand what a person in a wheelchair really, really experiences. So to understand someone, their situation, me Somayeh Malekian, myself, I have to go through that to understand it. Otherwise I can be an observer, a very good observer, a compassionate observer, but to totally understand it, I have to experience it.

I know it might be foolish in some situations; some extreme situations that I normally don't try. (Anecdote: I had a relative, and her son was trying to close the door. His fingers were at the door when he closed the door and he started shouting, crying, and the first thing that the mom did was doing the same thing to her hand to understand the level of pain that her son was going through. This is the most tangible way of describing it.)

What is it I'm trying to understand? By narrating, by talking to people as much as I can, it can help to put me in the similar situation that people have been through. You know, I have never been like my mom, not being able to go to school or not being able to leave her small village, as a kid, as a teenager, as a grown woman alone.

Of course, when I think about it now I understand it doesn't matter whether I am her daughter or a stranger. Seeing someone who can move freely with fewer obstacles than she has been through may trigger her jealousy. Now that is more human to me than feeling, simply, that my mother is jealous of me. Even those parts have become more humanized to me.

ST: Mahsa, you in particular seem to be struggling with this problem of forgiveness. As you're approaching your mother, learning much more about her life, even if tainted by her own reflections, perspective and control, she seems to still want control over her own narrative. You're questioning what forgiveness is. How do you think of forgiveness now, with what insight you've gained? What would forgiving your mother look like?

MA: Really, I tried a lot, I did. But it has always been something that we never talk about. The first time that my mom sent me her memories and whenever I try to talk to her, she becomes so defensive and it doesn't go on. I say, "Ok, sorry."

I don't know, maybe after this project I can start to try to forgive her, because it's something that doesn't end. Now I go visit with my mom and just one week is ok but after one week, all the things that I've been trying to push back come up. She herself hasn't been able to forget what she had been through when she was five. Forgiveness is not something easy, it's a healing process.

ST: How does it affect your relationship with your daughter?

MA: I've been trying to be exactly the opposite of my mom. But sometimes my daughter says, "You look exactly like my grandma, you are doing the same thing!" As I said, you can never be completely detached. My daughter, now she is a young lady actually, it seems that she can see the similarity.

ST: Our fate is to become our mothers. No, we evolve, but something is inevitable there, and it makes me think of what Somayeh was talking about with writing, narrating, talking with friends: the desire to change. The process of expression, expansion, the changing meaning on the page. I think it's a process of changing one's self. Is your attempt a desire to be personally understood?

MA: I think when you share your story it's not like saying, "People, look at me, I'm so miserable." It can help other girls, other women; so they can know that they are not alone. Actually, these were issues that Somayeh and I were talking about a lot: ourselves, our families, our ex-husbands, our memories. And it seemed that our families had a lot in common, therefore we had a lot in common. It attached us to each other: "Oh, there is some other girl that knows. She has suffered just like me." And it's very good to know that you are not unique, your pain, your suffering, is not unique, there are a lot of others out there. It can help you to cope, get over them.

It will absolutely help me because maybe I write just one page, 10 minutes, but I think about it for hours. I go deep in the thoughts and try to fix the little things that have been pushed away for so many years.

SM: This project has been something that we've been thinking about, talking about a long time. The topic and all that it involves. But now I found myself in total detachment with all that I had been trying to keep myself attached to.

I had left Iran several times, every time with hope and intention to go back, but this time it was different. I have the least hope of coming back currently that I've ever had, because of security reasons. So, somehow, it was a personal attempt for me to grab whatever I could. I wanted to tighten these ties. At the same time, from a journalistic point of view, in all my time covering Iran, I always had this specific interest in covering women. My challenge during these years has been that the women I would pick and the women my colleagues who covered Iran for western media would pick are normally middle class, educated women. Why? So many reasons.

First of all, they are easily found in Tehran. It's extremely hard for us to leave Tehran to other cities to cover stories because of the restrictions that the government put on us. That's the logistic part of the story. The other thing is about our audience in the west: they normally are more into the story that they can relate to, and they are the middle-class Iranian women, not the people like my mother. So I was thinking that this generation—the generation of our mothers—and also my generation who are not middle class, and are not living in the capital or other big cities, are sort of absent in the reporting, in the coverage.

In the past few years, there have been some memoirs that are written by Iranian women in the diaspora—there are so many of us around the world—but I felt still the generation of our mothers are categorized under this label of "exotic" or "mysterious" while to Mahsa and I they are totally human. They have normal intentions, normal aspirations, like any other person around the world, for what they do, what they like, how they want to get what they want, about their relationships with their children...

But all this said, the more I dove into the project, the more I realized it's not about the western audience, it's not about the absence of our mother's image in this big picture, and big puzzle. It's more about us. To understand, to find out more about the dynamics of power, how we both relate to our mothers, how both sides—our mothers and us—are trying after all these years to bridge the gap between us. Me by writing this, Mahsa by talking to her sister and reading through her mother's memoirs, which has been very tough for her. And our mothers, in their own way, are attempting to bridge this gap, and find new meaning after 30, 40 years.

❁

ST: We've talked about the pain involved in this process; it sounds like a painful experience for you both. In order to bridge the gap between you and your mothers, you and the rest of the world, you're drawing your own blood, which is somehow a position of strength. How did you get there?

SM: I want to give credit to the people we've been talking to. It wouldn't be possible without them. I've written memories that my mom has told me many times. But this time it was different. I could see that she was trying to remember her own childhood, I could see the desire in her tone, that she was excited and at the same time, at some points, regretful.

I think narrating—and I know I'm repeating this word, because it is empowering—narrating gives the person who talks the feeling of having agency. Yes, we can't have the power, the agency and the choice in our childhood, our education, our marriages. But now we are willingly and consciously making this choice to talk about what has happened to us and in this sense narrating is empowering. Then we can understand the level of responsibility that we did or did not have and also give ourselves some rights and better understand why we had certain reactions.

I believe that despite the pain, depression, and anxiety, those stories are still worth it because it helps us to understand, to push the walls surrounding us away, to create breathing space. The fresh air comes from different angles of these stories, theirs or my own. It opens windows that have been blurred, closed for years maybe, and now we're talking about it. I try to open those windows and give fresh air, more understanding, a bigger view.

MA: I remember Somayeh and I were talking about other women, how much we praised them, how successful they were, and comparing ourselves to them. I remember I told Somayeh that we are the kind of heroes that no one claps for. I said that we should never forget and when we compare ourselves with our situation and the hardship we have been through, then we feel less unsuccessful.

I think now that I'm writing this story and, more than writing, thinking about it all, I started to somehow appreciate myself more. I remember the past—it wasn't easy. Now, in my situation, maybe I'm not satisfied with it, I have a lot of dreams that may never come true. But what I've done is something that I should appreciate.

SM: Writing about this topic requires us to go back through memories with a very natural defensive mechanism, memories we have tried to forget, or we have tried to skip: patriarchal laws in our country that made so many troubles for us during our marriage and divorce, or bad memories we had at home, tough things we went through because of our parents, our mothers.

So we consciously decided to open that Pandora's box again and take every single item out, look through it and try to understand "Where does it belong?" Where can I put it back to be less annoying, and give ourselves that sense of self-appreciation that Mahsa is talking about?

ST: Is this the first time such a project—an oral history—has been possible in Iran, between Iranian women of different generations? It used to be that you were in the same house, or the same village, or it was passed down through skills rather than actual stories, but you are conducting formal interviews with women and family by phone, during a pandemic, amid famine and wars and other scourges of humanity. What tradition, if any, does it draw on? Or else what's revolutionary about it?

MA: I'm sure other people have tried it but I'm not familiar with it.

SM: I mentioned some memoirs by women. But the good thing about this project is that it's a shared attempt, Mahsa and I. Of course two people's experiences cannot generalize to all women in Iran but it has that sense of sharedness that we expect happens later for the readers as well.

ST: Yet something feels incredibly fresh here—what is the quality that is new? Is it technological? Is it political, or simply intimate, personal?

SM: All of these are part of it but none of them can hold the project on their own. There is a sense of self-awareness, self-appreciation among many of the working to middle-class women. People like Mahsa and I are not rare. There are so many of us who, after the Islamic Revolution, went to school, got an education, decided not to obey the patriarchal society's rule, and it really shaped a spirit and maybe writing this project can be a sign of how powerful this spirit is becoming.

Still, the toughest part for me is writing about myself here because there are so many things I doubt. People will read it and it's hard to be certain it's something I want to expose. That's the importance of it: people who have grown up in those circumstances coming to a level of confidence that they're prepared to talk about the journey from where they were to where they are now. This is the most exciting thing to me about this project.

SM: What Mahsa said about us as heroes and heroines who no one cheers—we are not just fighting against family and divorce laws in the Islamic Republic, we are fighting against those mindsets. Everyone would tell me that if you get divorced, and your father has a heart attack—he has a heart condition—then everyone will see you as his murderer. I was 22, 23 at the time and I said, "I can't bear that burden, I love my father, I don't want anything bad to happen to him." And I know those people who were telling me that were stupid people, but still it couldn't take all of the responsibility off my shoulders. It was like, "What if it happens, what if it really happens?"

That's just one part of it. Then think about your mother asking you just to stick to your marriage because everyone would see it as a failure, and after two, three years of fighting in the court I'm still trying to show that everything is normal to my mother—"I'm fine, don't worry"—because I didn't want to add something to their already heavy burden back home in Isfahan. So I would pretend that everything was fine and say, " I'm doing very well," even though I hadn't eaten in probably two days, not just because I was depressed but sometimes because I didn't have money. Or sometimes I didn't have a place to sleep, I would just backpack from this friend's house to that friend's house.

Actually, one of the points when I got closer to Mahsa was when I went to her place with my backpack—two shirts and laptop—I stayed there for a couple of weeks before going to another house. At the same time, I wouldn't let my family know the situation I was going through because if they knew they would say, "Why Tehran? Come home, stay with us, it's better than just living like a homeless person."

But living like a homeless person in Tehran was better for me than going back to my family, enjoying a warm meal two times a day. It wasn't easy to convince them that divorce was better than living a life of humiliation.

MA: I wanted to go to that part of my mom's memoirs that is related to revolution, and that year (1979), because I personally think they are very connected. I think the system unofficially gives authority and power and permission to religious families, to talk to their children with. It's somehow woven together. They know they have back up; the system is supporting their beliefs.

SM: After the revolution we had eight years of war, between Iran and Iraq, and our childhood and many other people in our generation's childhood was spent in the war. All of our childhood memories have something to do with war. The TV programs for kids were all about war, about morals and when we went to school they talked about the same things. This is what restricted our spirit of self-expression and our agency to talk about what we've been through.

The Islamic Republic system is in its weakest position in international relations now, totally isolated, bankrupt with all of the sanctions, and suffering huge waves of brain drain in the country. Now it's time for our generation to speak up. Our parents went through the revolution, now we are their children, revolting against them—Mahsa and I—by telling our stories.

ST: What is lost in translation?

MA: Every single word has its background that is part of the meaning. When you are not writing in your own language, there is always a risk of losing meaning but it is better than not communicating at all. I take interviews and notes in Farsi of course, and during translation I sometimes get stuck on a single word and think is it not the right word or not?.

SM: I'm thinking about the specific things that my mother has said. There are times in describing the situation, for example, when she remembered her father coming back from the mosque and she was listening to music on the radio.

What is lost there is the importance of the timing. My grandpa coming back from the mosque, doing something religious, something holy, and my mom listening to music which is a sin. And this contradiction, if I want to explain it, it's boring. Yet if I take it out, it's definitely lost in translation. Those more situational things are the most difficult. ✹

FROM OUR ARCHIVES

Excerpts from Stories about Children and Parents

A woman searching for a way to forgive her mother for having her ritually circumcised. A son's journey to his long absent father. A heroin addict's return home. A daughter trying to make sense of her father's slow descent toward suicide. Over the years, parents and children have been at the heart of so many of the stories we have published, first at The Big Roundtable and now at the Review. They are at once varied and similar. The circumstances change. The journey to understanding is eternal.

Damage
By Mariya Karimjee

Karachi, 1995

When I was seven years old and living in Karachi, Pakistan, my mother took me for my yearly check-up to the pediatrician. While I sat on a stool, polishing imaginary dirt off the buckles on my Mary Janes, my mother quietly asked the pediatrician if it was time for me to get the bug removed. The conversation wasn't entirely unfamiliar. Earlier that month, my mother had asked me if I was ever itchy or uncomfortable down there. I didn't understand what the questions meant, and I don't remember my responses. What I do remember is my mother explaining that around the time I turned seven, a bug inside of me would attempt to grow out of me down there and would crawl to my brain. It would need to be removed, she had said. After a brief examination, my pediatrician agreed.

A girl down the street that I'd grown up playing with had her bug removed, my grandmother told me. She was also seven, a few months older than me, and after she came home from the "operation" she felt so good that she was able to jump up and down on her bed. It was a story my grandmother told with gusto, and it made me itchy all over. I wanted this to be over and done with, to jump on a bed in unabated joy afterwards. Be gone bug, I whispered on the night before my operation.

My elder cousins, both girls, were each presented with a piece of gold jewelry when they returned home from their respective operations. Remembering this, I asked specifically for a simple gold chain with a teardrop pearl at the end. My mother's eyes filled with tears for a brief moment before my grandmother clucked her tongue disapprovingly.

I did not feel well enough to go around jumping on beds after my surgery. For two days I wore what felt unnervingly like a big-girl diaper, wet with blood. Peeing was so painful that I tried to last for hours without relieving myself, until my mother explained that I could give myself an infection. For the next year, I'd break out into a cold sweat whenever I encountered the kind-faced woman who'd laid me down on a tarp on her living room floor and spoken to me softly as she took a knife and cut me. I received the exact necklace I had requested, and wore it at almost every opportunity.

https://delacortereview.org/2019/01/22/damage

To read the full story, scan here:

Heroin: A Love Story
By Lisa Whittemore

In California, I had arranged to stay on my friend Audrey's couch. She would pick me up at Union Station in downtown Los Angeles then drive straight back to Venice. But first, as we pulled out of the station, 2,989 miles of road stretched ahead. My stomach fluttered with conflicting emotions. What I had done in Boston landed with a sickening thud by my feet, but I refused to allow my thoughts to drift over the past year. The taste of my own heartbeat, caught in my throat, was metallic.

I wished that I had the power to rewind and erase that past year—power I hoped to glean by shooting as much heroin as I wanted, unencumbered by the concern and stifling love of friends and family. How I was going to accomplish this was yet to be determined. But addicts are insanely resourceful, precise, and deliberate. I was no exception.

Heroin was my best friend. My only confidante. My road dog. My lover.

As the years began to slip by, the relief that heroin delivered would begin to dissipate. I would begin to question my loyalty to it, and to think about getting clean. Because drugs absolutely work—until they don't.

And I eventually would get clean, and have remained so for fourteen years. But that unshackling would not arrive for many more miles, many more years. On this seventy-two-hour cross-country bus trip it was the furthest thing from my mind. I did not use the time to reflect on my squandered life. I did not kick, as my friends had hoped I would. I did not plan to contact friends or family back in Boston once I arrived, to explain my abrupt departure.

I surrendered. I felt relief at my decision.

The other people on the bus were ghostly apparitions. Nobody rides across the country on that bus to make friends or enjoy the scenery. I spoke to one person on the entire ride, an older biker who once may have looked threatening, but now looked only weary. All his body parts drooped, heading south because that was the only way to go. He sat behind me in the last row with lank, greasy hair and a knotted moustache.

During our time together on the bus, we maintained a silent acknowledgment. We both knew, without saying so, that we were willing to sacrifice anything and everything on behalf of our relationship with drugs. Addicts share this sixth sense with each other. We also refrain from attempting to deter the course of addiction. Because we know there is no point.

In the triangular bathroom on board, I tried to fix. Setting up a spoon to cook, tie off, and hit a vein was near to impossible. Lurching over bumps I kept missing and making a mess.

The biker behind me noticed my agitated manner and my numerous bathroom trips. Wordlessly, he slipped valiums through the space between our seats. He had a mayonnaise jar full of pills. We had barely made a dent in them when he exited the bus in Las Vegas.

Pulling out of that Greyhound lot in Las Vegas, I smudged a circle into the dirt of the window with my shirtsleeve. I watched that old biker walk away. I felt envious of his anonymity. He lived a life free of emotional attachments. He answered to no one. He existed in a certain realm where invisibility was practically a requirement. I believed that what he had was all that I wanted.

https://delacortereview.org/2019/01/22/heroin-a-love-story

To read the full story, scan here:

Pupil of the Nation
By Diego Courchay

Two weeks before I went to visit him, my father set his hillside on fire. It began as a harmless clearing of weeds, turned out of control by drought and a broken hose. Now, on his isolated mound, scorched earth stood out like ink on a page. It showed the fire's progression in a winding semicircle around the house, having turned trees ocher as if by an early autumn. He had fought it alone, with a bucket, dozens of loads sizzling on advancing flames. It was still spreading as he threw the last of twenty gallons from the barrels of rainwater left from spring. And just as there was nothing left to do but wait and watch it burn, he saw the lights on firefighters' helmets, their trucks driving up the dusty road.

From atop his house, the landscape of forests and fields appears devoid of other homes, yet someone miles away had seen the smoke and called for help. It had not occurred to him to do so. In the end it was disaster averted; he escaped unscathed to tell the story, yet another tall tale about the crazy old writer cooped up in the middle of nowhere. People told him he was an idiot.

He told them that this is how life works: You get saved at the last minute and you go from tragedy to farce. That's how it went in the war.

The house where he lives on the hill was an abandoned sheep pen, perhaps more than a century old, until a sailor stranded himself on that arid land, and remade the house into a home with no ocean in sight. Jean Claude Courchay, my father, moved into the house some months after the sailor's death. He's another castaway with a seafaring past, who did his military service on the aircraft carrier *La Romanche*. Maybe somewhere in there is a common experience to explain the choice of home: two men who loved the sea retiring among the rocks.

The house is at the end of a dirt road on hunting grounds for boar, deer, and pheasant; winter buries it in snow, which melts and freezes the road into an icy slide that will discourage any car's descent. Until spring arrives, you can be isolated save for long excursions on foot or tractor. It's prime real estate to see the world recede into forgetting. A telling place, it speaks in its distance from all else, in age-old wooden beams and peace. But only if you can withstand the nights: those moments when you could believe you're the last person left on earth. My father had spent a long time looking for just that.

His home is a curious full stop for a lifelong wanderer. Then again, in traveling you must allow for your soul to catch up with you, as a wise woman once told me. For most of life, it's easy to imagine always staying one step ahead, easier to accelerate than to stop. This house is where Jean Claude stopped traveling fifteen years ago, long enough for his weary soul to finally find him.

Aloneness is a state unto itself. Strange things happen when there's not another soul for miles, when cities are a memory and the closest thing to a motor is the sound of boars plunging their snouts into furrows. A change came over my father in this remote life, one long sought and finally embraced. "I unfurl endlessly," he says, as his arms encompass the land. Living without interruptions, the soliloquy of self, that's when memories can surface. The past slips in; its murmur grows clearer. Stray recollections start to make their way home: Come right in, the doorway is no longer crowded by new experience.

Something there kindled his memory of the war, and I went back to listen.

It takes seven hours by direct flight from New York City to Paris. Once at Charles De Gaulle Airport, the next step in the low-cost trip southward is the train station Marne la Vallée Chessy, nineteen miles east from Paris, following the tourists heading for Disneyland. From there, the high-speed train takes slightly less than three hours and a half to Aix-en-Provence TGV station. Even when you disembark onto the sterile platform, you know you're in the south—the warmth, the landscape, and the sounds. The train continues to Marseille, but the city of Aix is still twenty minutes away by bus. That's where he's waiting.

We spend the night at a friend's apartment. I tell him why I'm here. The war, why not?

There's that time with the swastika smeared on the house, he begins.

No, I say, don't tell me yet; wait till we reach the hillside.

We take the morning bus to the valley, another three hours to Malemoisson, a stop on the edge of N85, where we're the only ones to get off the bus before it makes its way to Digne, the département capital, famous for being the starting point of Victor Hugo's Les Misérables. His jeep is in the parking lot nearby. Then we start the trip into the valley, the seven miles of winding road through fields and small towns, like traveling at the bottom of riverbanks with hills on both sides, heading upstream. A sharp turn left starts the climb before you reach the postcard town of Thoard. The road narrows; houses become scarce. After a couple miles, another turn left towards the hamlet of Les Bouguignons, past two houses and a chicken farm and onto a dirt road. Now it's stone, dust, and looming cypress, oak, pine, and mulberry trees for twenty minutes, steadily climbing a path that feels like one long bump. For years there have been car pieces strewn on the way, from those who braved the climb and from when the sailor drank himself into the countryside. My father has added a couple of oil pans, bits and debris of his own, paid in tribute to the climb, but the road he curses is his moat: It ensures no one will try to see where the path ends.

Then there is the house, above the lavender fields, the thick walls of stone. The key is hidden in a corner by the door, and once inside there awaits the large wooden table on the first floor, underneath those age-old beams he says make him think of a ship's hold. It's the best place in the world I know for conversation.

Once the wine is poured, he starts by telling me about the fire. The flames, the last bucket in vain and the firemen. By the time they arrived the base of the electric pole was burning—he concedes that would have been a bother—but the gas tank was still far off. Then again, salvation in the nick of time is what his life is made of. Though no one believes him when he says so, that's how it goes.

And to prove it, look no further than that morning in 1944. Then as now, disaster averted, and a wormhole in the conversation takes us back seventy-three years, to the moment that marked his childhood: "It's the same thing"—all seems lost and then, after the flames are spent, what remains is only a funny, self-deprecating anecdote over aperitif, something else to write about.

Except he never wrote about what happened during the war, not in full, not directly. In some thirty books of fiction and non-fiction there are tangents and fragments, but a man who made a living telling stories withheld this one for a lifetime. Until now he'd shared bits and pieces with me, memory flashes of littered ammunition, wartime deprivation, German soldiers, and ambiguity.

I first tried to write what little I knew six years ago and failed. "Your story is bullshit," he told me. "You don't get it." But you can only tell what you're told. Now the flames opened a clearing into the full story. So, we started talking last summer, a recorder between us, alongside the wine.

For a month he went back for me, to the period between 1940 and 1945, to the time that left scorched earth inside him that his memory traces like a finger upon a scar.

"Life is a series of ruptures and betrayals in which you end up alone. Since then I've always been expelled from everywhere; it's a vocation. There's no place where I've remained, and in the end, I find myself here," you tell me, and at the road's end, I'd like to know why.

It isn't really the war I'm after but the start of the flight. You were born in 1933 and lived many lives and left each one without seemingly looking back. Peace has come after you've severed all the ties. Never had a cellphone, never used a computer or the Internet; no TV, no one around, and goodbye to all that. Whatever keeps on happening out there in the world barely survives the climb. It took a lifetime to get this far, far enough. What propelled you here started when you were a child and your childhood was war.

Because I've come to learn that by the war's end, the die is cast: there will not be a straightforward life (if such a thing exists), instead the active rejection of one. There will be no belonging again, no being betrayed again. Fool me once…maybe once was enough.

When I was seven, my mother and I left for México, her country, and that past that crept at the edges, that blank instead of a family history on your side, became all the more foreign, an ocean apart. That started changing during a holiday in college. I found old black and white photographs in the trash, you put a finger on a soldier I'd taken out: that's your great-granddad. That's where I started to listen, trying to put the fragments together and failing. I hadn't learned how to ask.

When I finally did, something had changed; maybe it was all flooding back. You'd stored it away without ever fully closing the lid, memories still restless, half-buried, bubbling up. It happened at the beginning of your life, before you learned to dodge it all, a time when you were still unarmed. You can let go of people, but not of that.

- We talk about it because it interests you, but nobody gives a damn. This is seventy years ago, right? It's been pushed down for some time.
- But it's still stuck inside you, Dad.
- Because I've survived, while many in my generation are already dead.
- I remember you told me about it growing up.
- It's something that…when you're little, marks you for eternity. It's something I'll die with, I was nearly born with and I'll die with it. That's all.

We sit across from each other, you on a cushioned chair and me on a bench against the wall, near the sliding glass door where nightfall has subdued the distant woods, the large oak tree, and the trail left by the fire.

War? It was about time.

https://delacortereview.org/2019/02/23/pupil-of-the-nation

To read the full story, scan here:

Something More Wrong
By Katherine B. Olson

In the mornings, Creedmoor Psychiatric Center's Ward 3B resonates with a brand of white noise unique to a psychiatric hospital. It is loud with tinkling and crashing pumped in from television speakers: the metallic rush of the *Price is Right* wheel pulled by the show's spinning, smiling winners. Loud with the snores of still, slumped bodies in sticky vinyl chairs, with the shuffling of the 40 slippered and sneakered feet that pace between the two dayrooms, that wander around the nurses' station. Loud with the rollicking cackles of Caribbean therapy aides. With occasional outbursts over thefts real or perceived—"I wanna see her fit in a size 18! Let me see her breasts fit in my size 18 shirt. I wanna fucking see that right now, hippo!" Fights flame up and flicker out, undulating with moods, obscuring but never quite eclipsing the television and the miniature people who live so noisily inside it. The floor echoes with the game show announcer introducing his grand prize, a state-of-the-art home entertainment system. "If you're anything like us," he booms, "you watch a lot of TV!"

Alice Trovato watches a lot of TV. Sitting here, she looks like any other 52-year-old Queens housewife idling the occasional lazy morning in her living room to the soundtrack of soap operas and sitcoms. But Alice, clad in a navy institution-issued sweatsuit that stretches at the belly and tennis shoes that squeak across the linoleum, can be found here every morning dispensing wisdom to fellow inpatients, her surrogate daughters, from a chair she calls her "therapist couch."

Though Alice's skin is pallid and her cheeks sunken, her brown eyes are comparatively lucid in a room filled with women alternately sedated or enraged. She comforts Shania, who believes a bulldozer is parked inside her forehead, and Sabrina, who thinks an ex-boyfriend has taken custody of their nonexistent septuplet babies, whose names she cannot always remember but each of whom is called a different diminutive form of "Angel." She chides the woman called simply Rodriguez—who scratches and spits during fights and has an unnamed communicable disease the ward psychologist says "you don't want"—for disrupting therapy groups, and counsels Cynthia, an obese 20-something who hears voices, against her meal of Snickers bars—a meat patty, pastries, and Pepsi—even as chunks of cream cheese dangle from the girl's lips and bits of bagel fall to the floor.

The dayroom is not a living room and these women are not Alice's family—her own grown son and daughter live, as does Alice's husband, on their own on the outside. Alice's "daughters"—the three or four young women who call her Mama, waist-deep in depressions and psychoses similar to those Alice herself has battled, for a comparably shorter period, over the last five years—stroke Alice's scalp, tie her hair up for her in a tight bun, and unleash to her their problems, actual and imagined, comprehensibly or unintelligibly. She is the ward's elected president, a self-described advocate for those here contending with disorders she believes are more incapacitating than hers. Most days, she's feeling better.

Sometimes, though, angry voices and strange images emerge from the tightly folded recesses of her mind. Remnants of an abusive childhood, embedded in her memory the way accustomed-to house mice are in the walls of her old apartment, their presence, though once infuriating, forgotten until one scurries out from a hiding place, irrepressible, and she is forced to admit: "You're here for your own self, too."

Carla, an enormous young black woman, slumps in the corner, her head fully covered by a winter coat. Cynthia dozes off, drool collecting at her chin. Alice prods her knee to no avail. Friday is coming up, and Alice doesn't want Cynthia to lose the day's privileges: a trip to the Big Nosh, a food shop on the second floor that sells $2 pizza and, blessedly for Alice, caffeinated coffee.

Alice, and a few others, wouldn't draw a second glance on the bus or at the market, her illnesses almost as deeply concealed as they were throughout the first 45 years of her life: "Pieces of this were there, but it took building up," says the ward's psychologist, Dr. Yakini Etheridge, a woman in her early 30s with eyes that bulge behind glasses that slip down her nose. These pieces are easy for Alice to explain, harder for her to accept: Daily early-morning deadlines at work meant that she often spent just six hours at home each day. The children she had built her life around, her son and daughter (who, at 26, suffers from multiple sclerosis), had recently moved from home. Poor financial planning left Alice and her husband, an electrician, reliant on a state housing program. And ever-present though invisible, her abusive childhood, her physical ailments, and her as-yet undiagnosed mental illnesses hovered, amassing just out of sight.

"Why not practice half-smiling while listening to music?" suggests Etheridge.

"Everyone tells me that my smile is cute," says Sabrina. Alice agrees and smiles back as she always does, with her mouth closed. Alice's jowls droop when she talks, as though she doesn't have teeth.

Etheridge says, "It's nice to have a pleasant expression, even if you're not a smiler."

Carla wakes up, emerging from her makeshift sleeping bag to volunteer the group's closing mindfulness exercise: "We can go around and say how our weekend was."

Etheridge agrees—"My weekend was good," she says.

"I caught up on some reading," says the older white woman who is usually angry.

"I think you should skip me," says the other older white woman who is usually sad.

"I listened to Spanish music," says the girl who resembles a latter-day Michael Jackson. The next patient just giggles.

"I got a lot of work done," says Alice.

She reads, and writes dutifully in a journal she's kept since her early hospitalizations, which started after, at age 46, she tried to kill herself by jumping onto a subway track. ("My husband left for work. I didn't have the kids home. I just got up and took myself to the train station in Astoria and jumped on the tracks. It was weird," she says. Two men rescued her and she was taken to Bellevue.)

"And," Alice adds, "I visited with my husband."

He comes to Creedmoor because she won't, even on short visits, return to their home—a roach-and vermin-infested apartment they rent with government help. Social Security did not consider Alice's bipolar diagnosis a disability that would entitle her to financial support, but, with the schizoaffective designation, Alice's lawyer hopes she will soon receive disability, plus five years of back-owed support; she plans to use the money toward rent on an apartment in Middle Village, a predominantly Italian-American, working-class neighborhood. If there's any extra, she and her husband will put it toward a house upstate; for now, though, "we'll just need a one-bedroom; it's just us two, me and my husband. I'll buy a Jennifer Convertibles [pull-out sofa] for the kids, when they come over."

Alice's girls on the ward call her husband Dad, and give him candy orders. "Last weekend they ordered eight bags! He picked up chocolates, a People magazine one of the girls couldn't get her hands on, a crossword, a Sudoku, and a find-a-word. My husband's like, 'I'm not rich! But just tell them to give me a dollar-fifty and I'll pay the rest.'" He visits every weekend, and their children come every other weekend.

Etheridge finishes the mindfulness exercise with Sabrina: "I got to see two of my newborn babies, three and four months," Sabrina says. Alice looks down at her lap. Sabrina's delusion is persistent: She asked the treatment team about meeting with the chaplains. She wants to attend Protestant, Catholic, and Muslim services, because, a staff member explains, the clergy "are the only ones who believe she has children."

This is not a bad place, not the hell it had been, historically, or the caricature constructed in horror films. Etheridge goes as far as to call it a "positive place, a place of rehabilitation, arts and music, beautiful and bright," and, in one sense, she is right. There are places to go to pass the time: There is 102, the newly-renovated annex attached to the main building that houses a weight room, basketball court, and bowling alley; and the Big Nosh, the food shop on the second floor run by mentally-disabled workers. There is natural light here, almost wherever the patients go, except for the nurses' stations, which somehow seem to always have the dim, artificial lighting of a Holiday Inn corridor.

https://delacortereview.org/2019/01/22/something-more-wrong

To read the full story, scan here:

The Boy Who Lived
By Douglas Mine

I don't love Theo because he's fleet of foot, or uncommonly coordinated. Or because he's comely and smart. I love him because he's my son, and because he's Nicoletta's son. I don't love him more than I do Bruno or Joseph or Tobias. But it's different. Over the past two and a half years, as I approached and passed sixty, I've developed a tenderness for and devotion to our fourth boy that sometimes—quite often, really—feels like rapture.

Some of it has to do, I guess, with his handicap, and how stalwart he has been in overcoming it. But I'd already learned firsthand (Joe had open-heart surgery, at Miami Children's, when he was six) that ailing kids are inherently brave in a way that comes off looking like heroism to us grown-ups. Their fortitude does have an element of innate valor, but it's also composed of a child's innocent ignorance of what he or she is in for.

In a way not intended by Wordsworth, I think Theo in some fashion has been father of the man who engendered him. In that he, unwittingly, taught me something. In truth, he's still teaching me, because I haven't got it thoroughly figured out, and probably never will. But he provided me with something fascinating to keep thinking about. You see, there were points there a few years ago when it felt to me like Theo's coming along was about the worst thing that could have happened, because its consequences seemed to be endangering the most valuable thing in my life: my marriage. At the lowest moments of the reproach I was feeling—for Nicoletta but also for my weak and doubting and spiteful and inadequate self—it seemed to me my wife and I were in peril of breaking apart.

But what has happened over these past couple years is that the worst thing has become the best thing. Theo makes me laugh several times every day and fills me with a kind of quotidian bliss that I'm certain is rare among my contemporaries. I am in some ways in decline and half-jaded, like they are, by accumulated decades of endeavor and success and failure. But I've been presented by this child with a delectable conundrum, one that compels me to try to account for how it is that the direly negative can become the exuberantly positive, how what seems like a disaster can amount in the end to a glorious sort of exaltation.

https://delacortereview.org/2019/01/22/the-boy-who-lived

To read the full story, scan here:

The Man That Wasn't
By Karla Bruning

When I was six years old my best friend's father killed himself. I remember overhearing my mother on the phone—things I wasn't supposed to hear. Something about bloody glasses. Something about a gun. I didn't know what it all meant until my mother sat me down. Suddenly, I was terrified that my dad would kill himself, too.

I remember standing on the entry stairs of the split-level home that my mother, my sister, and I had moved into just a few months earlier. With my parents freshly divorced, my mother had to pare down. Gone was our sprawling suburban home, tucked into four acres in the woods at the terminus of a dead end. Now we lived in a neighborhood where the houses were so close together that they had no windows on the sides.

I stared at my dad, who had come in the front door. My mother had called him at work because I was so upset. Winter was settling into Chicago and the trees behind him stood naked, braced against the wind and cold. My father, in his suit and cashmere coat, knelt on the step below me, so that we were at eye level.

"What's the matter, kiddo?" he asked me, as he placed his ape-like hands on my shoulders.

"Daddy, I don't want you to die," I cried. "I don't want you to kill yourself."

"Karla, I'm not going to die," he said.

"Promise. *Promise* you won't kill yourself," I said.

"I promise you," my dad said to me, looking me in the eye. "I promise you I will never kill myself."

I didn't believe him.

Too frightened to let him escape my sight, I went to work with him that day. We visited a wire factory where my father had a client. I hung onto my father's coat as we walked through the cavernous warehouse, cold and gray like the sky outside. A man at the factory gave me a spool with red, green, and gold insulation wire woven around it, like shiny, moldable thread. It was November, but the batch date on the top of the spool read "6/25/84." I played with it. I stroked the ridges of the wire, cool and prickly against my skin. I put it in my nightstand along with my rosary, prayer books, and piggy bank—prized possessions. And I saved the spool, because it reminded me of that day. It reminded me of my father's promise.

He broke that promise. He just did it slowly.

https://delacortereview.org/2019/01/22/the-man-that-wasnt

To read the full story, scan here:

The Big House
By Claire Sudduth

I'm not from Mississippi but my father is. His mother grew up in Greenwood, a small town about fifty miles east of the Mississippi River, where the flat Delta land is just beginning to tilt and roll again. Her name was Vernon—an unusual name for a woman, made even more unusual because no one in our family can remember how she got it. The story I've been told is that Vernon was named after an itinerant preacher who traveled through Greenwood sometime in the 1910s and swept her mother into a fervent, if brief, religious frenzy. Vernon hated her name and told her children never to pass it on. But then she died. She walked outside one Sunday morning in 1974, picked up the newspaper, took it back to bed with her, and that was it. The maid found her two days later, a cold cup of coffee still on her nightstand. She was fifty-six. Her oldest child, my father, was twenty-five years old and two weeks into his first job at a bank up north in Chicago. I came along many years later and so my (middle) name is Vernon too.

My family is deeply, intractably Southern. I'm not. I'm the only one on either side (my mother comes from Memphis) born above the Mason-Dixon line, a fact that inspired my parents to affectionately dub me "The Damn Yankee" whenever I said or did something they considered too Northern, such as pronounce "New Orleans" as two separate words or say "you guys" instead of "y'all." For the past nine years I've lived in New York City, working at magazines and renting charming (OK, cramped) apartments—a lifestyle about as far removed from the Mississippi Delta as one can get while still remaining in the United States.

Still, I feel culturally connected to the region, much the way I imagine children of immigrants identify with a homeland that has never been their own. I don't know why I feel this way, exactly. It's a hard thing to suss out. Maybe it's because before New York, I lived for seven years in Nashville. Or that on more than one occasion I've had to explain to fellow Northerners what pralines are. Or that when I take those "soda or pop?" regional dialect quizzes, the language algorithms never know where to place me. I grew up accompanying my parents to places such as Graceland and Vicksburg's battlefields. On a family trip to Natchez when I was six or seven, I bought a small Confederate flag in the gift shop of an antebellum home-turned-museum and kept it in my room, on display next to some plastic horse figurines, until I grew old enough to know what it meant and put it away.

But while I feel drawn to the South, my father has taken pains to scrub his Southernness away. He lost his Mississippi accent decades ago; when the bankers and businessmen in Chicago heard his drawl they assumed he was uneducated and maybe a little stupid, so to further his career he worked to get rid of it. Only a few traces remain, such as his habit of shortening the name of his home state to three syllables instead of four. Or the words "pin" and "pen," which he vehemently believes should be pronounced the same way. And then, of course, there's the biggest relic of all: Cotesworth, the grand, gable-roofed white mansion and accompanying nine hundred-and-some-odd acres that members of his family—Vernon's family, my family—has lived in for more than 150 years. My dad calls it the big house.

Cotesworth is one of the Delta's last remaining plantations. My great-great-great grandfather, a man named James Zachariah George, bought it, named it, and used the land to grow cotton, wheat, corn, oats, rice, hay, and sweet potatoes. He was also a lawyer, then a colonel in the Confederate army, the chief justice of the Mississippi Supreme Court, and for two terms, until his death in 1897, he was a U.S. Senator. He believed in slavery. He fought against Reconstruction. When the political tide turned away from him, he devised methods to ensure that his people—white people—would remain on top. In 1931 the state chose him as one of two Mississippians it wanted to memorialize in the National Statuary Hall in Washington D.C. You can still find him there, bold and bronze, with one hand in the breast of his overcoat, right in the U.S. Capitol's visitor's center.

J.Z., as my family calls him, raised his nine surviving children at Cotesworth. When he died, he gave the plantation to one of them, who gave it to another, and so on. Today it's a cattle farm. Vernon's younger cousin, Kat, still lives there. Kat is eighty-three now but she still wakes up before dawn to feed the two hundred or so cows that graze on Cotesworth's fields. She drives a tractor and bales her own hay, but she's been having a harder and harder time finding the money—and energy—to keep up the big house. Sometimes she'll rent it out to Hollywood filmmakers, which is how Cotesworth came to be Jessica Chastain's great mansion in *The Help*. But maintaining such an old house costs a lot of money and there just aren't enough movies filmed in rural Mississippi to pay for its upkeep.

Every time I visit Cotesworth the paint is peeling a little more, the floorboards sagging a little lower. The house still doesn't have central heat or air-conditioning, and the second kitchen—built in the 1950s, when Kat and her late husband, J.B., moved into the place—has been plagued by wasp nests for as long as I can remember. So in 2013, Kat sold Cotesworth to the state of Mississippi. She moved out of the big house and into a much smaller one elsewhere on the property. The state, through a non-profit, will preserve the mansion as a museum and event space. Kat is the last person who'll ever live at Cotesworth.

There are two sides to the story of Cotesworth, but they both start the same way: with the man who owned it. Everything happened because of him.

https://delacortereview.org/2019/01/22/the-big-house

To read the full story, scan here:

Last Trip to Quetico
By Jim Doherty

When we get to Monument, we see no signs of recent use. Jimmy does the horse work again, hoisting the canoe and a pack while his gimpy client plods along behind with lighter stuff. The famous portage turns out to be not a big deal. At the other end, we find an official keep-out notice nailed on a post with a handwritten postscript, in red ink, exempting Quetico-bound parties. Who knows when that qualifier was added?

Lovely, river-like paddle en route to Saganaga, but a nasty wedge of black clouds is coming after us. Wind picks up. "Looks like we're in for it!" I holler. "If we get caught in the middle of Sag when that baby hits, we're toast! You know what they say about lightning and boats. Maybe we should pull over now and wait it out."

Jimmy shrugs. "Nah, we'll be okay," he says. "We can take shelter if it gets bad. Not to worry."

He's right. The storm passes. No problem. Arrive mid-afternoonish at the same campsite we used the first night out, and find it just as we left it, the pile of firewood intact. Finish setting up before the rain starts and retire to our respective abodes, him to read, me to catch up on notes.

I'm beat and he is, too. Break camp, two portages, a long paddle, make camp…a lot of work.

So. We're almost done. Out my tent "window" I see grey sky and grey water separated by a thin black band of terra firma. Rain pattering. Jimmy clearing his throat. Otherwise, not a sound. Perfect silence. Cherish it, Dude.

I don't go in much for reflection but every once in a while I do get caught up in the moment. Such as now. For Jimmy, this is just the end of another Quetico trip but for me it's the end of the line. My paddling days are over. Hell, I'd only be fooling myself if I thought otherwise. If I tried again next year, chances are I'd end up busting something a lot worse than my tailbone. This is what people mean when they say growing old is all about letting go. Sooner or later, every superannuated voyageur has to call it quits and now it's my turn. Sad? Yes and no. Growing old is about acceptance, too, and we Midwesterners are pretty good at that. Not surrendering, or giving up. Just having the grace to realize when it's time to stop being a burden and get out of the way.

We all know there's a last time for everything but so often in life we don't recognize one as such until long after it has passed—the last conversation I had with Gram, the last time I took Mom out for a drive in the country, the last time I read "The Night Before Christmas" to the kids. This one I do recognize. I've pretty much understood all along this will likely be my farewell canoe trip and that has focused my mind. Been paying close attention. Haven't missed much. My notebook's full. Long after we've hauled out and strapped the canoe back on top of Jimmy's van, I'll continue to appreciate what we needed to do to get here. Not just the paddling, but everything else, too. This is a gift, one that in no small way helps ease the loss.

https://delacortereview.org/2019/01/22/last-trip-to-quetico

To read the full story, scan here:

IMAGE CREDITS

Zenique Gardner Perry: pp. 32; 52–53.

Eléonore Hamelin: back cover illustration.

Somayeh Malekian: pp. 54; 91–97.

Simpleinsomnia: cover, "Children posing on a porch with their toys," edited from the original. https://www.flickr.com/photos/simpleinsomnia/19215171739 Licensed under Creative Commons 2.0 https://creativecommons.org/licenses/by/2.0; back cover, "Nude black baby on a couch," edited from the original. https://www.flickr.com/photos/simpleinsomnia/12624476474 Licensed under Creative Commons 2.0 https://creativecommons.org/licenses/by/2.0.

Lawrence Tabak: pp. 30–31.

Mitch Wolf: p. 10.

ABOUT THE AUTHORS

MAHSA AFARIDEH, is the pen name of an Iranian poet who lives in Tehran.

ZENIQUE GARDNER PERRY writes stories about family, race, faith and all its intersections. She is also the co-founder of Undo Bias, a group that guides organizations in moving towards antiracism. Zenique is an MFA Candidate at Washington University in St. Louis, where she lives. You can find her on Twitter @Zenique_GP

SOMAYEH MALEKIAN is an Iranian journalist who has covered Iran for American media since 2010. Prior to that, she enjoyed teaching English in several villages and towns around Iran for 10 years. Currently, she is an associate producer at ABC News international bureau in London.

LAWRENCE TABAK attended Northwestern University and the University of Iowa, from which he holds a BA and MA. His essays and articles have appeared in numerous publications including Salon, themillions, The Atlantic Monthly and The New York Times. His novel, In Real Life, was published in 2014 and his newest book, Foxconned, an exposé on economic development as seen through the Foxconn in Wisconsin fiasco, releases this month from the University of Chicago Press. He is based in Madison, Wisconsin.

ABOUT THE DELACORTE REVIEW

Stories do not write themselves, much as writers may modestly insist they do. Stories exist because writers need to tell them—a need so deep that they will endure false starts, woeful sentences, dead-end paragraphs, two-dimensional characters, flabby prose, wrong turns, and shaky narratives. In short, they will risk all the things that, taken together, comprise the writer's greatest fear: failure. Specifically, failing to tell the story they need to tell.

The Delacorte Review (https://twitter.com/DelacorteReview) believes in writers, and what they can accomplish when unencumbered by anxiety, terror, despair, and fear of rejection. We believe that writers—both emerging and experienced—who feel supported and confident can produce their best work, and that readers benefit. We want our readers to discover new, original works of ambitious narrative nonfiction, often by writers they are reading for the first time.

Core to our mission of creating a home for writers and readers is our newsletter, Writerland (https://thedelacortereview.substack.com), an ongoing journey to finding joy in writing. Because nothing good ever came from writers punishing themselves.

If the best fiction is propelled by imagination, we believe that the best narrative nonfiction is propelled by the relentless and often-lonely business of finding out things that are often maddeningly difficult to find. In a word: reporting. Nonfiction storytelling can be as compelling, riveting, and transporting as fiction—so long as you come back, as they say, with the goods.

If there is a story you need to tell, perhaps we can help you write it (https://delacortereview.org/submissions).

The Delacorte Review appears four times a year and is published in cooperation with the Columbia Journalism School (https://journalism. columbia.edu) and The Delacorte Center for Magazine Journalism. *Please support our mission: discovering real true stories and how they happen.* https://journalism.givenow.columbia.edu/?alloc=25454#

MASTHEAD

Founder and Publisher: Michael Shapiro ✉@ShapiroMichael

Editor: Mike Hoyt ✉@MichaelHoyt

Senior Editor: Cissi Falligant

Managing Editor: Selin Thomas

Associate Editor: Claire Fox ✉@ClaireFoxes

Staff Writer: Natasha Rodriguez ✉@NatashRodriguez

Podcast Producer: Katie Ferguson ✉@MakaFerg

Illustrator: Eleonore Hamelin ✉@LeoHamelin

Website Design by Mario Garcia ✉@DrMarioRGarcia and Andy Rossback ✉@ARossback

Art Director: Joan Hacker

ADVISORY BOARD

Daniel Alarcón, Helen Benedict, Jelani Cobb ✉@Jelani9, Samuel G. Freedman, David Hajdu, LynNell Hancock, Marguerite Holloway, Dale Maharidge, Alissa Solomon, Jonathan Weiner

Published in cooperation with the Columbia Journalism School and The Delacorte Center for Magazine Journalism

2950 Broadway, New York, New York 10027

Dean: Steve Coll ✉@SteveCollNY

Director of The Delacorte Center: Keith Gessen ✉@KeithGessen

Copyright 2021 © The Delacorte Review

https://journalism.columbia.edu

www.delacortereview.org

Note: Before there was The Delacorte Review ✉@DelacorteReview *there was The Big Roundtable, which between 2013 and 2018 published works of ambitious narrative nonfiction, many of which can be found on our Archive page.*